DATE DUE

Also by the same authors

Cool Careers for Girls with Animals

Cool Careers for Girls in Computers

Cool Careers for Girls in Engineering

Cool Careers for Girls in Health

Cool Careers for Girls in Sports

IMPACT PUBLICATIONS I

COOL careers

for girls

in *food*

Ceel Pasternak & Linda Thornburg

Library of Congress Cataloging-in-Publication Data

Pasternak, Ceel, 1932-
    Cool careers for girls in food / Ceel Pasternak & Linda Thornburg.
        p. cm.
    Includes bibliographical references (p.).
    Summary: Profiles eleven women who work in various food service professions, including chef, food critic, preparation artist, food scientist, and health food store owner.
        ISBN 1-57023-127-3 (hard) -- ISBN 1-57023-120-6 (soft)
        1. Food service--Vocational guidance--Juvenile literature. [1. Women food service employees. 2. Food service--Vocational guidance. 3. Vocational guidance.] I. Thornburg, Linda, 1949-   . II. Title.

TX911.3.V62 P37 1999
647.95'024--dc21

                            99-043040

                            CIP

Publisher: For information on Impact Publications, including current and forthcoming publications, authors, press kits, bookstore, and submission requirements, visit Impact's Web site: www.impactpublications.com

Publicity/Rights: For information on publicity, author interviews, and subsidiary rights, contact the Public Relations and Marketing Department: Tel. 703/361-7300 or Fax 703/335-9486.

Sales/Distribution: All paperback bookstore sales are handled through Impact's trade distributor: National Book Network, 15200 NBN Way, Blue Ridge Summit, PA 17214, Tel. 1-800-462-6420. All other sales and distribution inquiries should be directed to the publisher: Sales Department, IMPACT PUBLICATIONS, 9104-N Manassas Dr., Manassas Park, VA 20111-5211, Tel. 703/361-7300, Fax 703/335-9486, or E-mail: coolcareers@impactpublications.com

Book design by Guenet Abraham

Dedicated to all those past and future,
mostly uncelebrated women who have created
delicious food in the kitchens of the United
States. There is a need for culinary historians
to look for the lost voices of women
cooks and the dishes they invented that
fill the pages of our cookbooks.

Contents

A Special Introduction from Les Dames d'Escoffier International

Les Dames d'Escoffier International is dedicated to supporting and promoting the achievement of women in the culinary professions and to fostering excellence though educational and charitable activities. With active chapters throughout the world, Les Dames d'Escoffier works to enhance the professional lives of women in the food, fine beverage, and hospitality industries.

We are very enthusiastic about your interest in a culinary career. Food is the biggest business in the world, and about one fourth of all working people in the United States are employed in the food industry. Think about how your own family buys food and you will begin to get an idea of the scope of the industry and the variety of jobs to choose from. A trip to the grocery store would not be possible without the farmers who grew the food, the companies that processed it into the products on your grocer's shelves, the buyers and distributors who arranged for it to end up in your grocery store, and the retail merchants who sell it to you.

But the grocery store is only one of several places where your family gets food. There are also restaurants, health food stores, street vendors, institutional kitchens such as your school cafeteria, and places to eat in airports, hotels, trains, and on cruise ships. All of these places offer possibilities for rewarding employment. For those want to work with the wealthy, the career of personal chef also is a possibility.

Besides eating food, we love to talk and write about it, so there also are plenty of jobs as magazine editors, food writers, restaurant critics, cookbook authors, food stylists, photographers, television personalities, and culinary educators. And we love to celebrate with food, which means there are opportunities to cater parties or plan events at which people eat and drink.

The food industry is composed of some giant companies, but many more small companies. It is a good place for those people who want to run their own business. In this book, the authors show you many small business owners who have used their love of food as a starting place for creating companies where they earn a good living, have fun working with food, and create jobs for other people. You'll also learn what it's like to work for a company, and you'll get a taste of what it's like to pursue a food career in the armed services.

There are many schools that offer training in food preparation and for food and hospitality careers. A good place to find them is in the ShawGuides. Established in 1988 as a publisher of comprehensive worldwide guides to creative career and educational travel programs and creative career programs, ShawGuides has offered free online access to the unabridged, continually updated content of each guide since 1995 at (http://www.shawguides.com) One well-known school is The Culinary Institute of America, which offers programs that lead to a bachelor's degree, an associate degree, or a certificate in both Baking and Pastry Arts Management and Culinary Arts. The Institute also has a program for high school students called Career Discovery, which covers industry trends and basic cooking methods and how to organize professional equipment.

The Culinary Institute of America divides food careers into broad areas—entrepreneur, manager, food writer, food stylist, caterer/event planner, culinary educator, and product development specialist. Let's use these same divisions to talk more about the opportunities in the industry you might have not realized are available.

Entrepreneurs need to combine marketable ideas with ambition, business savvy, and a lot of hard work. Managers (who can work in many different jobs, including director of sales and marketing for a resort, general manager of a four-star hotel, corporate food service director, or restaurant consultant), need expertise in purchasing, costing, the front (customers) and back (operations) ends of the business, marketing, computers, human relations, menu development, and management. Food writers and editors need strong writing skills, knowledge of culinary principles, and familiarity with current consumer and industry trends. Food stylists artfully prepare and arrange food with appropriate props for still or video photography. They could work for magazines, newspapers, corporations, cookbooks, catalogs, television, and in the movies. Food stylists need to be artistic, precise, patient, and versatile.

Caterers and event planners work closely with their clients to custom design events such as weddings, business receptions, art gallery openings, or intimate dinner parties. Along with menu planning, food preparation, and service, caterers may be responsible for the entertainment, decorations, staffing, invitations, equipment rental, sales, and billings. For this type of job you need superior planning and organizing skills, to be able to work well under pressure, and to know how to run a business. As a culinary educator, you could work in high schools or colleges or teach continuing education classes to adults. You could also offer workshops and classes for food lovers. Culinary educators need enthusiasm, strong leadership and people skills, and professional experience in the course of study to be taught.

Culinary research and development (R&D) specialists such as food scientists and food technologists work for food companies to create new products and product lines, evaluate ingredients, and ensure that products meet company standards for flavor and quality. R&D specialists also might develop and test recipes for magazines. You need creativity, a working knowledge of food chemistry, and a good sense of the consumer market to work in this field.

Getting Started Now

This book is a great place to start researching food careers. The stories of the women will give you a good idea of a typical day on the various jobs and the challenges and rewards of the many different ways to work with food. You will also learn how some women made their career choices. Along with each story, you will find a checklist with some clues about what type of personality would be suitable for a particular job. Information about salaries is also provided.

The final chapter, Getting Started on Your Own Career Path, gives you advice about what to do now, identifies helpful and fun reading materials, and lists organizations you may contact for additional information. Some have local chapters and some offer scholarships. Like Les Dames d'Escoffier, these organizations are there to provide help and information. Make sure to use these great resources.

COOL
careers
for
girls

in food

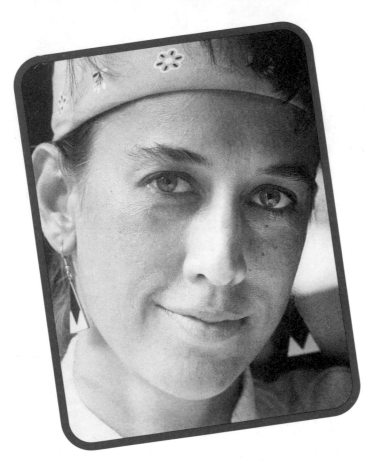

Susan Spicer

Susan Spicer

Chef and Co-owner of Bayona

Owner of Spice, Inc., New Orleans, LA

Chef, Restaurant & Cooking School Owner

She Puts the New in New Orleans Cooking

In a city known for its delicious, spicy food, it's easy to remember this famous chef's name—Susan Spicer. Called one of America's most exciting and talented chefs, she describes her cuisine as "contemporary global" or "New American."

Susan has a reputation for eclectic interpretations of classic dishes at Bayona, her restaurant in the French Quarter of New Orleans. Her modern American cuisine has international flavors drawn from Italian, French, Asian, and New Orleans creole influences. Signature dishes include sautéed salmon with choucroute (sauerkraut) and gewurztraminer (wine) sauce, described by one restaurant critic as "the briny fish playing exquisite counterpoint to the tangy

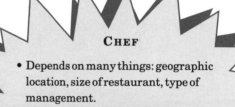

CHEF

- Depends on many things: geographic location, size of restaurant, type of management.

- Entry level, gets liveable wage; higher wages when have management responsibilities like sous chef.

- Chef, from $30,000 to $150,000 and higher.

- Extra income from restaurant ownership, teaching, cookbooks, television shows.

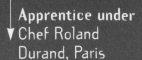

Helps friend catering out of house

Apprentice under Chef Daniel Bonnot, New Orleans

Apprentice under Chef Roland Durand, Paris

choucroute, the whole lavished by a satiny buerre blanc infused with the spicy, flowery essence of the wine."

"Some of my specialties," says Susan, "are an appetizer of eggplant, caviar, and olive tapenande that is full of the earthy accents of the Mediterranean. Also a goat-cheese crouton with shiitake and oyster mushrooms in Madeira cream. To our grilled shrimp we add black-bean cake and coriander for a dash of Southwest flavor. We do a flash-grilled tuna that has a lively hoisin dipping sauce for an Eastern touch. A standard is our velvety cream of garlic soup. We also do a white bean, sage, and prosciutto soup."

"I love this work. It gives you immediate gratification when you see those clean plates coming from the dining room. You know people like your food. But it is demanding because you are only as good as the last meal you prepared."

First chef job at
Savoir Faire

Travels to California,
Europe

Gains fame at
Bistro

A Seven-Day Work Week

Susan's typical work week is a full seven days, with her time split between the restaurant and her cooking school and retail gourmet store, Spice, Inc. She usually starts her day about 10 a.m. at the store, helping the manager do whatever needs to be done. Her main responsibilities are to promote the business, help with catering orders, and run the cooking school.

"A lot of customers asked me to do cooking classes. New Orleans is insular in terms of our cuisine, so available classes before were for jambalaya, gumbo, things like that. I teach my style of cooking, and I also bring in local people and people from out of town to teach classes. I get to meet these other chefs, see what they do."

Susan tries to get to Bayona before lunch is over and works through the afternoon and evening, leaving for home around midnight. Since she teaches on Tuesday night, she takes that day off from the restaurant. Sometimes, when she has a special private lesson scheduled, she'll open the restaurant, work there all day, then teach in the evening.

Susan plans to hire help at the store. "I discovered that I am a workaholic," she says. "But we do take vacations. We close the restaurant for 10 days in August, and we're deciding whether to close the store. My boyfriend, who is manager of the store, and I want to go to Europe for a week or 10 days, so we're figuring out how to arrange that."

Raised on New Orleans Food and Music

Susan is the daughter of a U.S. naval officer father and a Danish mother. She moved to New Orleans when she was six. She never planned on being a chef, "but my mother is a great cook, and I love to eat." As a girl, she thought about being a detective (she loved the Nancy Drew mysteries) or going into the music business. She liked swimming and hanging out with her friends. "My father called me a responsible child, not a thing you want to be called. But I do take on responsibilities for things others might not pay attention to, and that helps now in my work."

Susan enjoyed languages, and took one year of Spanish and four years of French in high school and in college. "I left college after one year because I was really 'fuzzy' about what I wanted to do. My friend Pamela drew me into cooking."

Susan's friend was catering out of her house and asked Susan to help her. Then the young women decided to take jobs in a small restaurant kitchen to improve their skills. But that didn't last long. "They told us we had bad attitudes and let us go."

Pamela lined up a job in the kitchen of an elegant restaurant, Louis XVI. Chef Daniel Bonnot agreed that

Pamela could hire Susan as her assistant if an opening became available. Then the lunch cook quit. "It was my first real job as a cook. It was stressful, but I found I really enjoyed it. The stress was too much for Pamela and she left." It was 1979 and the start of Susan's career.

Chef Daniel took Susan on as an apprentice and later was her mentor. She was a lunch cook, then did appetizers, and in a couple of years had worked up to sous chef (assistant to the chef), running the restaurant in the daytime. "Daniel was a great mentor. He inspired me, pushed me. We had terrible fights because he'd tell me to do something and I'd say I didn't think I could, and he'd say shut up and do it. He had more faith in me than I did myself. We are still good friends."

Daniel "pushed" Susan into her first chef job when the owner of the Louis XVI was looking for someone to run the restaurant of a hotel he had bought uptown on Saint Charles Avenue. Susan, who had just returned from a summer apprentice-

CAREER CHECKLIST ✔

You'll like this job if you ...

- Develop a taste for food flavors

- Enjoy the activities and camaraderie of the kitchen

- Will learn math, how to write, and another language

- Enjoy it when people like your cooking

- Pay attention to details

- Will learn business skills

- Want to 'stand out,' will keep improving

- Like to teach

GROUNDBREAKERS

Most Popular Cookbook a Joy

The renowned cookbook *Joy of Cooking* was privately printed in 1931 and has been in demand ever since—being revised and reprinted for 43 years.

It was a family affair from the beginning. The recipes and instructions were written by Irma von Starkloff Rombauer (1877-1962) of St. Louis, Missouri, who came to cookbook writing after the death of her husband in 1930. She was 54 years old. Her daughter, Marion Rombauer Becker, tested the recipes and illustrated the book. The mother and daughter team worked together to continually revise and make the book relevant and up-to-date. In 1951, Marion became coauthor, taking on more responsibilities. Marion's husband John helped with the writing; her sons contributed as well. She wrote, "Ethan contributed his cordon bleu and camping experiences; Mark, his interest in natural foods."

After Marion's death in 1976, no new work was done until the new book, when Ethan carried on the tradition with the help of his wife, Joan, and son, John; his brother, Mark, and Mark's wife and son. This book is called The All New All Purpose *Joy of Cooking* by Irma Von Starkloff Rombauer, Marion Rombauer Becker, and Ethan Becker.

ship in France, opened Savoir Faire in the fall of 1982.

Paris and Chef Roland Durand

Susan got to go to Paris on a 10-day promotional tour because Daniel couldn't go. "The Hotel Sofitel Paris brought in musicians and a guest chef to feature the food and music of Louisiana. I was so excited about what I saw there. We worked in a big kitchen that served several restaurants. I made friends with some of the guys, speaking my college French, and wondered if I could ever apprentice there. They told me to ask the chef. I finally worked up my nerve the last day of the tour and spoke to Chef Roland Durand. He said I could, and we arranged it for the summer of 1982."

Susan enjoyed that summer. She stayed in a small room designed for apprentices and got her meals and a very small amount of pay. "I learned technique and appreciation for ingredients like mushrooms and squid, which were not readily available in New Orleans. And I got a chance to compare my knowledge with others. The levels of expertise are called

most things were plated in the dining room, to individual plate presentation done in the kitchen.

With her increased confidence, Susan took on the responsibility of

For me, this work gives immediate gratification. I love seeing all those clean plates return to the kitchen.

apprentice, commis, premier commis, chef de partie, and sous chef. By the time summer was over, I felt I was at the chef de partie level—I could run at least one part of the kitchen. The experience gave me confidence, because I had really only worked in one restaurant."

That year was also a time when nouvelle cuisine was in full swing—a change from classic French, where

the new Savoir Faire. "It was a hard learning position—besides the food, you are putting a crew together, hiring and firing. At first, I took it personally when people quit. I felt like a mother hen with chicks leaving the nest. I've learned that people come and go, and I don't own them. Still, it's hard because you build rapport and form a bond, especially working so closely with the sous chef."

Susan left the job in 1985 because she was pressured to do more Cajun and creole dishes. "I was kind of restless, so I took a road trip to California. I interviewed in a lot of kitchens and restaurants that I couldn't afford to

Greece, worked in a little restaurant, and went to Italy. I had a good time working and traveling. I was a little shy of saying 'I'm a cook, can I come in and look at your kitchen?' so I didn't go into as many kitchens as I might have."

On Her Way to Fame

Susan returned to New Orleans, worked in the kitchen at the Meri-

Taste your ingredients to check them out before your start making anything. And taste as you go along. Have high standards and pay attention to detail.

eat in. I came close to working for Chef Joachim Splichel, whose work I still admire, but I got a chance for a free trip to Europe."

The trip was to a jazz fest in Nice. "You cook for 10 days straight and are paid cash. So there I was in the south of France with 1,200 bucks and a return ticket in my pocket. I went to

dien Hotel, then left in 1986 to open the tiny 40-seat Bistro at the Hotel Maison de Ville. Soon dinner reservations became hard to get as word spread about Susan's tasty cooking. "My customers started telling me I needed a larger place. Some offered to invest if I would open my own restaurant." One day a "regular customer" told Susan he had just bought a place that would be perfect. She went to look and fell in love with it. Her investors/customers then went to look and agreed. So Susan and Regina Keever became partners and Bayona opened in 1990.

With solid support from her customers, local publications, and food critics, Susan and Bayona began getting national attention from magazines—*Gourmet, Bon Appetite, Food & Wine*. Food critics, and readers' polls have named Bayona one of the top places to dine in the United States, in the Southeast, and in New Orleans. Susan received the James Beard Award for Best Chef Southeast Region in 1993. She has been the guest chef at famous restaurants around the world, appeared on television, and contributes her talents to numerous charity events.

In a commencement speech at The Culinary Institute of America's main campus in Hyde Park, New York, Susan advised, "Always maintain a solid work ethic. Take your time to learn as much as possible early on, because those are the things that will stay with you. Never settle for the status quo. You always have to try to do more, be exceptional. It's very competitive out there. You have to stand out. But you have to do it because you want to do it."

Paula Lambert
Paula Lambert

Cheesemaker/Founder/President, Mozzarella Company, Dallas, TX

Major in History and Elementary Education; Master's Equivalent, Italian Language and Art History, Universita per Stranieri, Perugia, Italy

Cheesemaker
Entrepreneur

A Classic Approach to Cheesemaking

In 1982, Paula Lambert began making fresh mozzarella at a small Dallas, Texas, cheese factory. She called it the Mozzarella Company. Today she employs 17 people, and the company ships mozzarella and other cheeses all over the United States to restaurants, specialty stores, and individual homes. She began her business by selling her cheeses to the owners and chefs of a number of the best restaurants in the Dallas area.

Paula speaks Italian, which she needed when she wanted to learn the art of cheesemaking from Italian masters of the craft. She also speaks Spanish, which she uses to communicate with her Spanish-speaking workforce. She also needed to understand the people in Mexico who taught her how to make Mexican cheeses—after

ENTREPRENEUR EARNINGS

People who start their own business may not earn any salary in the beginning. They invest their own money in the business, they get more money through loans or venture capital, and, until they make a profit or "go public" by selling stock, they probably pay themselves a small salary and put profits back into the business to help it grow. Sometimes when they sell the business, they sign a contract that pays them executive compensation to stay and manage the company.

she had perfected the Italian ones. Her days are filled with supervising a staff of cheesemakers, order takers, packers, and shippers, and with marketing of her line of cheeses. These include several varieties of mozzarella and also mascarpone, queso blanco (traditional Mexican cheese), ricotta, caciot-

ta (Italian style country cheese), and other unusual cheeses made with either cows' or goats' milk. Today, you can buy more than 30 different cheeses from the Mozzarella Company.

Day Begins at 4 a.m.

The cheesemaking process begins at 4:00 a.m. every day. Milk is poured into stainless steel tanks and pasteurized. Cultures and enzymes are added to coagulate the milk. The result is curd, which is cut into squares; the curd and whey (the watery part) separate as they are stirred. Then flavors are added, if necessary, to make a certain type of cheese. Cheese is stored in big refrigerators until it is ready to ship.

"When I first started, I did all of the

Gets married,
▼ works in husband's
business

Learns
▼ cheesemaking from
experts

Opens the
▼ Mozzarella
Company

activities that go into making cheese," Paula says. "But the nice thing about owning your own business is that you can design it so that you do what you like to do. Today I am more involved in administration and the public rela-

tional Women's Forum. Her visibility in the community is good for business. She also is active in a number of organizations connected with food, among them the International Association of Cooking Professionals and the Ameri-

Cheesemaking requires good math skills. For example, you have to know how to calculate the proportions of ingredients to add.

tions aspect of it. I love to meet people. The people who work for me do the cheesemaking now."

Paula devotes lots of time to her community activities. She serves on a number of Dallas community boards such as Uptown Dallas Public Improvement District Board of Directors and the Dallas Chapter of the Interna-

can Cheese Society. Before she began making cheese, she was even more active on Dallas community committees and boards, including the Junior League. Her experience as a volunteer gave her some of the organizational skills that she needed to start her business.

To succeed as an owner of a small

business like Paula's cheese factory, you have to be a problem solver. Paula had to creatively solve all the problems that presented themselves as she tried to make her dream of cheese-making a reality. "I was very determined and persevered. Things don't always go as you plan. You have to find ways to get around problems. You can't just give up when you run into problems."

Inspired by Italian Mozzarella

Paula taught first grade after she graduated from college, and then had studied the Italian language and art history in Italy. On a later visit to Italy, she was eating some cheese and it dawned on her that cheese-making would be a good business to be in. She had been working with her husband in his landscape architecture business, but she wanted a business of her own. Paula thought making fresh mozzarella would be a business that could succeed in Dallas, because at the time no one was selling it there.

Paula needed to find space and acquire money for equipment and supplies. She convinced two friends to become her "silent" partners. Together they invested more than $100,000 in her idea. Next, Paula had to decide what sorts of cheeses to make and learn how to make them. She was able to convince a cheese-maker from a little cheese factory where she bought cheese in Perugia to call a famous Italian cheese professor he didn't even know and ask how she could get lessons on making traditional Italian cheese. The professor recommended an expert, and this man came to the United States to teach Paula to make cheese. Paula felt it was important to get classic training from the best—the cheesemakers of Northern Italy. Later, when she wanted to make Mexican cheese, she adopted the same approach—she went into Mexico and learned from the best Mexican cheesemakers.

Solving Problems

To make the classic Italian cheeses, Paula had to find a source for milk. Because you can't buy large quantities of pasteurized milk that isn't homogenized (you can't make cheese out of homogenized milk), she had to buy raw milk and pasteurize it herself. But, there are different ways to pasteurize (heating the milk to destroy harmful bacteria without altering its chemical properties). Paula wanted to use the method that resulted in the best flavors for the cheeses. You need to use a slower pasteurization method to make the

CAREER CHECKLIST ✓

You'll like this job if you ...

Can get along with others and have leadership skills

Can persevere and find ways to solve problems

Can be a good public relations spokesperson for your ideas

Will learn and can find the expert to teach you what you need

Will develop business skills

Are good in math and languages

GROUNDBREAKERS

Frozen Food, a Woman's Idea

Mary Engle Pennington (1872-1952) was appointed Chief of the U.S. Food Research Laboratory and served from 1918 to 1919. In charge of food handling and storage, she devised methods of preparing, packing and storing food to prevent or retard spoiling, including the then-new technique of freezing. She established standards for railroad refrigeration cars. From 1919 until her death she worked as a consultant to private industry.

best cheese. Less of the bacteria that give cheese its distinctive flavor is killed with slower pasteurization.

Paula bought used equipment from a friend who had had an ice cream factory, and he helped her design her cheesemaking plant. Paula would get up at 4:00 a.m. every morning and go buy the milk from a nearby dairy farm. The cheese maker from Italy wrote the recipes in Italian, and Paula translated them into Spanish so her Spanish-speaking workers could follow them. The separation of the curd from the whey and the shaping of the cheese is done by hand, which makes a better cheese. Through trial and error, Paula and her workers eventually began making great mozzarella.

But that was half the battle. Now she had to find people to buy the cheese. Regular grocery stores didn't want the product because it had a short shelf life and, since it was expensive to make, it would be too expensive to sell when they added their mark-up. So Paula began knocking on the kitchen doors of good hotels and restaurants. She found

that cooks were quite interested in using fresh cheese in their recipes, and that gave Paula the start she needed. As more cooks used her cheese, her reputation grew, and she began sending it to restaurants in New York and Chicago as well as selling it in Dallas. The number of cheeses grew as well, to include cheeses that would make good selections in specialty gourmet stores, where the short shelf life and the

higher price weren't as important as the fact that the cheese tasted so wonderful. Today, Paula sells to many gourmet stores, as well as to restaurants.

By the time Paula had been in business for three years she had American chefs talking about her, and the Mozzarella Company was on its way to making a profit. She had entered contests and won, and she displayed her cheese at a convention of young American chefs. Articles were written about her in many food magazines, and she won several food awards. Chefs from all over the United States began ordering her cheese. Because it had to be delivered fresh, she shipped it directly to them.

One of the secrets to Paula's success is her focus on her customers. "It's so much easier to keep an old customer than to get a new one. We try to please them. But sometimes you also have to be tough. When I first started, I remember a chef who made me cry because he was so harsh in his criticism." In 1998, the Mozzarella Company made more than 250,000 pounds of cheese. When she started in 1982, she sold 100 pounds a week.

Education Plus Business Skills

Paula grew up in Fort Worth, Texas, the daughter of a father who was an attorney and a mother who did volunteer work. "I was a happy-go-lucky child. I was in Campfire Girls and I loved to swim. In fact, I won lots of medals for my swimming as a teenager. I also liked to cook. I remember I made cakes in tiny pans when I was younger. My grandmother was a great cook, and my mother loved to go to cooking classes."

Sent to a Wisconsin prep school for high school, Paula went to an all girls' school in Virginia for her first years of college, where she took American Studies. "That was good for me. We could excel without worrying about what the boys thought. I would rec-

ommend that any girl consider an all girls' college, because it is a wonderful time to focus on your studies and what you want to do with your life."

Paula finished her education at the University of Texas at Austin and graduated with a degree in History and Elementary Education. Her first job was teaching first grade, which was good preparation for teaching her staff how to make cheese, she says. She

met her husband, Jim Lambert, in Italy and married him shortly thereafter. For a number of years she helped Jim run his landscaping business in Dallas, where she learned some important concepts about running a business, including bookeeping.

When she was ready to start her own business at the age of 39, she had a number of important skills—knowledge of two foreign languages so she could learn from the masters, teaching skills so she could work with her staff, organizational skills she gained from running community events, and knowledge of business, which she gained from working in her husband's company.

Bonnie J. Alton

Bonnie Johnson Alton

Owner, Bonnie's Neighborhood Bread Business,
Great Harvest Bread Company, St., Paul, MN

Major in Speech Communication

Bread Store Owner

The Generous Baker

Bonnie Johnson Alton is a 'morning person.' That's the time when she has the most energy and zest, which fits perfectly with her business as a baker of bread.

Bonnie's Neighborhood Bread Business in St. Paul, Minnesota, opens at 6:30 a.m., but some of the staff arrive as early as 5:00 a.m. to start the day's baking. Bonnie likes to be there to open the shop, and she usually stays until the lunch-hour rush is over around 2:00 p.m. During the mid-afternoon hours she has some time to herself—doing home chores, running errands, giving attention to the other things in her life. Before the shop closes at 6:30 p.m., Bonnie checks in. After closing, a staff person lets Bonnie know how much bread is left over. Before Bonnie

- Technically skilled workers can earn from $9 to $13 per hour plus health care and profit-sharing benefits.

- Customer service workers can earn from $5.50 to $11 per hour.

ENTREPRENEUR EARNINGS

People who start their own business may not earn any salary in the beginning. They invest their own money in the business, they get more money through loans or venture capital, and, until they make a profit or "go public" by selling stock, they probably pay themselves a small salary and put profits back into the business to help it grow. Sometimes when they sell the business, they sign a contract that pays them executive compensation to stay and manage the company.

retires for the night, she gets on her computer and uses a spread sheet to figure out what quantities they should bake for the next day. She faxes it to the store so the next morning the crew will have their bake orders and know what to do.

"I'm an urban farmer. Rather than 'going to work and leaving work,' I have a life that requires that I get certain things done in order to be happy—work at the store, family time, household management time, personal leisure time. These things change daily—sort of like the seasons—and I love it."

Bonnie's Bread Is Special

Bonnie's store is a Great Harvest Bread Company franchise. "We're a whole wheat bread bakery. Our commitment is to use traditional scratch baking methods. We mill all of our own flour with stone mills that are like those used during the past two centuries (although now they are powered by electricity). We use ingredients as close to their original form as possible—honey, cold compressed yeast, raw nuts and seeds, and dried fruits or the highest quality frozen fruits."

The work at Great Harvest stores is

Joins small firm,
marketing and
traveling

Learns
about small
business

Works for large
company, knows
it's not right place

done in the front of the store, where customers can watch staff mixing and kneading the loaves. "We can visit with customers while we work and easily move forward to the counters to wait on them. My friends will sometimes drop in, bringing me a cup of

coffee. I'll take a break to visit for a while. They know I can't really get away in the morning to come and visit them."

Bonnie's store is one of 200 businesses located in a three-mile area on Grand Avenue—a shopping destination for people who enjoy the area's many restaurants and mostly locally owned shops. "We spent a lot of time selecting our location. This area serves the needs of local people for groceries, banking, dry cleaners— all their errands—and it attracts shoppers from outside the neighborhood."

The breads and cookies Bonnie bakes attract the customers, but it is the customer service that brings them back. "Each person coming into the store gets a free, generous slice of bread. We've been here five years now, and we're close to our cus-

Enters partnership, learns bread making

Opens bread business

tomers. We've watched children grow, learn to walk and talk. We celebrate people's lives."

Customer service and a spirit of generosity are attitudes that Bonnie has insisted on in her business. The

thing is in the oven), they can move to the second task and don't have to ask a manager or supervisor 'what do I do now?'"

Making the breads runs on a clock-driven schedule and is quite physical,

> A lot of math is involved. We work with base 10 (dollars, decimals), base 16 (ounces), base 4 (quarts), base 60 (minutes).

24 people who work in her store (7 full-time and the others part-time) range from gray-haired senior citizens to high school students; they are hired as much for their attitudes as for their abilities. "Everyone has two tasks assigned to them, so if there is a slow time on the first task (like every-

although machines do the real heavy work. "It's a team effort. I tell the staff 'You can't do it, but you and two other people can. You can't clean up the back, wash dishes, and wait on customers.' But the three of them can figure out who does what for what length of time (like 'I've been working with the customers for the last 2 hours and I really need a break; I'll sweep and you work the counter')." Bonnie emphasizes to her workers that it's okay to ask for help. "It is not a sign of weakness, but it identifies areas that need emphasis. It helps us do our best and have fun doing it."

Passion for Food

"I grew up in a family of cooks in Bagley, Minnesota, and I was always in the kitchen with my mom. She was a teacher of home economics and science and a great American cook. My maternal grandmother fixed wonderful Scandinavian food for us." Growing up in the 1950s, Bonnie rebelled as a teenager. "I became the gourmet cook of the family, reading cooking magazines and making my family eat lots of strange things. As an adult, I enjoy eating wonderful foods in restaurants and then attempting to create those things in my kitchen."

In her bread store, Bonnie has added some products of her own and shared them with other Great

CAREER CHECKLIST ✔

You'll like this job if you ...

- Are an early morning person
- Love bread products
- Enjoy people and want to give good service
- Are optimistic, have a good attitude
- Will learn the math and business skills
- Are not afraid of hard physical work
- Love to learn
- Are willing to take risks
- Can solve problems, make decisions

GROUNDBREAKERS

She Founded Pepperidge Farm

Margaret Fogerty Rudkin (1897-1967) was a baker and entrepreneur. When searching for additive-free bread for her asthmatic son, she developed a stoneground wheat bread. In 1938 she decided to make it a business and founded Pepperidge Farm Baking Co., which emphasized natural, healthful ingredients. It became a million dollar business which still exists today. In 1963 she published *Margaret Rudkin's Pepperidge Farm Cookbook*.

Harvest Store owners. She loves her grandmother's Christmas cake, called Julekaka. Over the course of a couple weeks, she experimented with making the recipe wheatier and in large quantities. "It is a big hit for us. We sell it during the Thanksgiving and Christmas seasons." In addition to whole wheat chocolate chip and whole wheat peanut butter cookies, the store sells a traditional scone, whole wheat cinnamon rolls, and 'scruffins,' a scone-muffin combo filled with marionberries. "We also have savories, like you might find in a French pastry shop. I'm not a sweet eater, but I like different flavors in food, and I like small amounts of food that I can just grab and run with. For example, we've made a rolled up swirl with sun-dried tomatoes, herbs, and parmesan cheese."

Lifelong Learning

Although Bonnie loved food, she did not think about a career in the field. She graduated from college with a degree in Speech Communication.

Her first job was doing public relations for a nonprofit organization, then she did PR and marketing for several small companies.

Most of her work experience, which prepared her for her bread-making business, came during the years she worked alongside the owner of a small

and learned to stay focused and optimistic about what I could control, while not losing sleep about the

things I couldn't control. I honed my skills in marketing and in understanding what mattered to my customers."

firm. "We provided training for lawyers. I traveled around the country marketing our courses and lining up the law professors and lawyers who would teach." Bonnie learned how small businesses function. "I became fluent in the ups and downs

Seeking a personal change, Bonnie was hired as director of marketing for a large law firm in Minneapolis. There she encountered her greatest frustrations—too many people helping to make what seemed to her simple decisions. She began thinking about what she really wanted to do. Her training had prepared her to own a small business, and her passion made her choose a business in food. When Tom and Sally, who owned a Great Harvest Bread Co. in Minneapolis, were looking for a partner to open a store in St. Paul, Bonnie asked to be considered. "It was serendipity. I loved Tom and Sally's store and their bread. We were a perfect match as partners. They had the technical skill and demonstrated success; I had the passion for the product,

weekends with Tom and Sally, she learned the processes of bread making. She quit her job in 1994 and devoted a couple of months to preparing the store for opening—buying equipment, fixing the space inside, and hiring and training staff. In March, 1994, the store opened.

A Good Neighbor

Bonnie gives back to the community that has helped make her business a success. Donations to running and

You also have to know business math, determine the cost of ingredients, and figure out the best pricing structure.

the marketing experience, and willingness to take the risk."

By taking a loan from the profit-sharing savings account established by her long-time small business employer, Bonnie was able to fund her share of the business. By working

biking events, sponsorship of an annual high school invitational swim meet, and supporting the local library volunteers are a few examples. Recently, St. Paul's Greening the Great River (the Mississippi) Project was given 500 cookies to help feed volunteers on a tree-planting day. "In a small way we help nonprofit organizations do more by offering the gift of hospitality—nutritional food for their volunteers, sustenance with a little bit of our hearts in each bite."

Bonnie lives just six blocks from the bakery. She recently married Brian, a

ride, visit friends, or attend community events. But by 10 o'clock, urban farmer Bonnie has faxed off her bake orders to the staff for the next day's baking and gone to bed. She's got to be up early to open her store.

Baking is a blend of science and intuition. Science helps us understand how things work together chemically; intuition helps us feel for the right texture, look for the right color and know it's right.

lawyer with a commercial law practice only 4 blocks away from their home. "We have a blended family— Joe and Charlie are Brian's teenage sons, who live with us half the time. My daughter, Medora, and her husband, Paul, are recent college graduates." Bonnie and Brian find time in the early evening to take walks, bike

Julia Iantosca

Winemaker, Lambert Bridge Winery, Healdsburg, Sonoma County, CA

Major in Fermentation Science

Winemaker

A Blend of Science, Art, and Intuition

Julia Iantosca works with all phases of winemaking—from checking the grapes on the vines in the fields to overseeing the bottling of the finished wine. She is the winemaker at the Lambert Bridge winery in Healdsburg, located in northern California's Dry Creek Valley, Sonoma County. Because the winery is small, producing only 20,000 cases, Julia has direct involvement with every aspect of the business.

"What I love about this work is the camaraderie, being part of a gracious and helpful community of people. When someone has a problem or needs help, especially on the production side, people share information and equipment. Wine is a satisfying product to produce. It is very tradi-

WINEMAKER

- Entry level $30,000
- Experienced, depending upon size of winery $60,000 to $150,000

JULIA'S CAREER PATH

Active in 4H, plans to
▼ be a vet

Interns at Dry Creek
▼ Vineyards

Graduates college,
▼ marries Robert

tional. Although there is obviously a potential downside since it contains alcohol, its history is enjoyment at table, a gracious way of dining."

Spring Growth, Summer Harvest

The growing of grapes, called viticulture, is a seasonal process. Julia's job varies, depending upon the time of year. In the spring, the growth is just beginning. "Part of my job is to be sure that the vineyard manager, who is the expert, tends to the vines properly. I keep an eye on what will be the harvest."

In the winery during spring, Julia blends the red wines from the previous year's harvest. "I hire a winemaking consultant and use her as a sound-ing board. With merlot, we have grapes from several different vineyards, so each batch will have a slightly different taste. We also use a blending variety like cabernet franc and a blended cabernet sauvignon. We have 18 different wines on the lab counter to taste. As we taste the wines, we talk about what should mix with which. We are trying to achieve our Lambert Bridges style. That is, a complex flavor that is fruit driven and characteristic of the individual variety of the grape."

In the summer, Julia prepares for the harvest. "We hire a couple of students to intern and help." Although there are several winemaking schools in the United States—in California, Washington, and Oregon in the West; New York in the East—students from

Australia, New Zealand, and South Africa are sometimes more available for hire because it is wintertime, not harvest time in their countries.

Dressed in a tee shirt, shorts, and tennis shoes or rubber boots, Julia is out in the fields almost every day checking the grapes. She determines when to harvest at each vineyard, usually during late August through October. "Leading up to the decision, I check a combination of factors. One is the physical condition of the vines. Two is the chemical analysis—we check the sugar level, the acidity, and the pH level. Third, I taste to get the flavor of the fruit."

Julia also takes into account the weather. Will a heavy rain damage fruit? Will it stay cool longer? Will it get too hot? Also since the winery is a business, Julia schedules the picking dates so there will be steady work for the winery employees but they won't be overworked.

"There is a window of opportunity, but nothing is perfect in agriculture. In 1997 we had an enormous harvest and brought in far more fruit than we could handle normally, it was ripening so rapidly. At harvest, everyone works seven days a week, 12-hour days, sometimes longer. That harvest was really crazy."

Once the grapes are in the winery, things begin to slow down, although there is a lot of work tending to the new wine. Julia resumes her regular hours, usually working from 8:30 in the morning to 3:00 or 3:30 in the afternoon. December is generally the quietest month. During January and

February, the finished wines—merlot, zinfandel, chardonnay, and sauvignon blanc—are blended and bottled.

wine. "If you pick too soon, the wine is green, thin, and not too flavorful. If too late, the wine is too high in alcohol."

Julia also makes stylistic choices to affect the taste. "The sauvignon blanc, if picked at a lower sugar, tends to be more green, grassy, and herbaceous in style. If you wait for riper, more sugar level, the taste will be more mellow, with a citrus aspect to it. Neither one is wrong, just a preference of style. Each winery wants to have its own signature, so making those choices gives the winery its own style."

The Taste is Science and Art

The picking date and ripeness of the fruit directly impact the quality of the

Julia purchases the barrels in which to age the wine, another decision affecting taste. "We buy about 350 a year from various producers here and in France. Each has a house style which gives a different flavor. The interiors of some barrels are slow toasted over a small fire, some are quick toasted over a hot fire."

"My job is a combination of science, art, and intuition. We are trying to have styles that are fruit driven, characteristic of the personality of each individual variety, and complex. I work very hard to be sure the wines are soft, supple and mouth filling. For the sauvignon blanc, we ferment in barrels rather than tank. During the aging process the wine sits in contact with the yeast, called leaves, that is fermenting the wine. Through the aging we stir the yeast back into the wine and get a gradual breaking down of the yeast cell, and get a little bit of flavor from that."

Wanted to be a Veterinarian

Julia grew up in Somis, a town of 800 people in southern California between Los Angeles and Santa Barbara. Ventura County is known for

CAREER CHECKLIST ✓

You'll like this job if you ...

- Can focus on details like aroma, flavor

- Have an interest in agriculture

- Like to work outdoors

- Are organized and detail oriented

- Can take responsibility and make decisions

- Can motivate people

Origins of California Wines

In 1779, Franciscan missionaries planted the first vinefera—the European species of wine-grape bearing vine—in California. The vines passed from the missions to small growers in and around Los Angeles, where most people lived then. In 1847, when California was annexed to the United States, wine growing began to spread. Following the gold rush of 1849, people and grapes moved north to the San Francisco area. Sonoma County, one of the larger northern coastal counties, became the center of winemaking by 1900.

Sonoma Valley had the last of the Franciscan missionary vineyards—one of the earliest commercial vineyards north of San Francisco (General Mariano Vallejo appropriated the Franciscan plantings) and the first great winery name of northern California—Buena Vista. Its Hazell Vineyard started the rush to using French oak barrels to age California wines and thereby revolutionized their style, especially chardonay's.

Source: The Oxford Companion to Wine, Jancis Robinson (Ed.). (1994). NY: Oxford University Press.

its citrus, avocado, and row crops like lettuce and broccoli. Julia and her cousins rode horses and were active in 4H. By age seven, Julia had decided she wanted to be a large animal veterinarian.

"I never had any meat animals in 4H projects. My folks knew it would be too hard for me. But my cousins did. I remember my cousin's first lamb. You have to show them, so we used to walk it with a dog collar and leash. We both just sobbed when it was time to sell it."

In high school, Julia worked hard because she knew there was a lot of competition to get into vet school. "You got teased if you tried hard. It's sad but true. I was in some honors classes where everyone was trying hard, but in my regular classes I was teased. But I'm just ornery enough I kept at it."

Julia entered college at San Jose State planning to become a vet, with her major in microbiology. She knew she wanted to do something in science, in case she didn't make it into vet school. She transferred to University of California at Davis because she wanted less clinical lab work. Then she took some wine cours-

> When at age seven I said I wanted to be a veterinarian, no one ever said girls don't do that. My parents' attitude was, 'You can do whatever you want to do. The limits on your dreams are self-imposed.'

es just for fun and got captivated by it. To be sure she'd like the industry, she arranged an internship at a winery.

"The school had a planned educational leave program. You stayed enrolled in college and got credits for time spent in an internship. I talked with my advisor, then wrote letters and called on wineries to ask if I could do an internship. I interned at Dry Creek Vineyards. Afterward, I had to write a paper about my experience. I

LAMBERT BRIDGE

1997

Zinfandel

DRY CREEK VALLEY

79% ZINFANDEL
15% CARIGNANE
6% PETITE SIRAH

ed dating. When they married, they moved to the Sierra Foothills, and both worked at Stevenot winery. "We moved to an area where we didn't know anyone, and we worked together. It strengthened our partnership—we've been married 20 years now."

Motherhood and Work

Julia and Robert moved back to Sonoma County and both got winemaker jobs. They selected a house half way between her job in the northern part and his in the southern part of the county. "We chose Sonoma because it would be easier for us both to get winemaker jobs where there were a lot of wineries. It was a bit difficult to have a family. When my daughter Catherine was born in 1991, I took eight weeks' maternity leave, but after two weeks I was going in once a week to write work orders. You can't just get a 'temp' worker to fill in for you in small

discovered I really liked the industry. I met a great group of people. So I abandoned my dream of becoming a vet."

Julia met Robert at Dry Creek. She went back to school for her senior year. After her graduation, they start-

to check on how things were going. My husband was busy with his job at his winery. You just do what you need to do."

Learning physics is important, it helped me understand how the equipment works—grape presses, separators, pumps, bottling. It helps to have some mechanical aptitude.

business. I carried my daughter in with me and worked for a couple hours while she slept."

In November 1995, Julia's daughter Elizabeth was born during a record late harvest. "I was writing a work order for the crews on my way to the hospital, and on the way home from the hospital, I stopped by the winery

Rena Pocrass

Founder, President, and Co-owner, Chocolates à la

Carte, Sylmar, CA

Chocolatier

She Transforms Chocolate into Art

It was the challenge that attracted Rena Pocrass to the world of chocolate—the challenge to create wonderful, unique shapes using exquisitely tasting chocolate. "I bring the 'Wow!' to the food, because first you eat with your eyes."

Rena has designed chocolate sunglasses for actor Jack Nicholson's party, a nautilus shell for a Nancy Reagan luncheon, and saxophones for one of President Clinton's dinners, in addition to the many small cups, cones, and other containers used for desert creations.

It all started in the early 1980s. Rena's friend Sharon Meresman dropped off a box of chocolates in different shapes and a brochure about a special chocolate mixture that easily melted and reformed so you could

ENTREPRENEUR EARNINGS

- People who start their own business may not earn any salary in the beginning. They invest their own money in the business, they get more money through loans or venture capital, and, until they make a profit or "go public" by selling stock, they probably pay themselves a small salary and put profits back into the business to help it grow. Sometimes when they sell the business, they sign a contract that pays them executive compensation to stay and manage the company.

- Workers in a chocolate/candy factory earn minimum wage to $30,000.

Source: Encyclopedia of Careers and Vocational Guidance

pour it into forms or molds. Intrigued with the idea of molding something edible, Rena thought, "This could be a great business."

Rena's friend went away on vacation, but Rena began researching her idea. "I'd get up about 4:30 a.m., California time, do my household chores, then get on the telephone to the people in the East for information. I found out where to buy the molds and the chocolate and how much they cost. I found a California distributor. When my friend got back I had all the information we'd need to start."

The two women started the business, Sweet Fantasies, in Rena's kitchen. "I do not remember how much money it took to buy the molds and the chocolate compound, but it was not much," she says. "Sharon

Starts making
▼ molded chocolate

Opens Sweet Fantasies
▼ store in Encino

Takes job with
▼ food stylist

was the detailed, business person; I was the visionary, idea person." They began by selling to friends, then school events, then charity events.

Bob Hope Meltdown

For a golf tournament in Palm Springs, Rena and her partner created chocolate caricatures of comedian Bob Hope, "ole ski nose." In their booth between sun visors and water coolers, sales were okay, but they hadn't figured on the desert heat, so things got rather soft. "This was a learning experience for me. I'm basically a shy person, but I found I could put myself out with people I didn't know because I was so enthused about our product." One beneficial result—a retail shop owner in Palm Springs arranged to sell their chocolate.

As sales grew, the two women decided to open a retail shop on a main street in Encino. They hired a crew of teenagers (ages 16 to 18) to work at the counter and in the kitchen in the back. But when the year's lease came up for renewal, Rena's partner decided that she didn't enjoy the business, and they weren't making enough profit. She wanted to quit, and Rena didn't want to buy her out; they closed the business.

"I realized that I preferred to sell to businesses rather than the public. It would be easier, because if you sell to one corporate person they can generate a lot of business, but you have to sell to hundreds of consumers."

49

Develops Bear Paw Shell in own kitchen

Starts own business

The Visual Effect of Food

Rena next took a job with a food stylist who worked for advertising agencies. Rena realized while assisting on production sets how important the visual presentation of food was and that a lot of artistic talent was involved. She also met lots of society people and made contacts in the food industry.

unique, three-dimensional designs that would wow them." Rena created a shell-shaped bowl that would hold ice cream and had height. "I realized that I had a great presentation for the banquet industry." Then Rena once again began to research.

Rena found out costs and worked "backwards." She researched what banquet caterers charged for deserts (about $3.50 or $4) and figured they

> I was always sitting back and watching. I'm a shy, reserved person, but I got over it because I'm so enthusiastic about what I'm doing.

"I realized that I wanted to make art with chocolate. I wanted to create

took a 50 percent profit, giving her a cost range of $1.75 to $2. She estimated that the caterer's labor cost 30 cents and ice cream 28 cents. That meant Rena could charge 80 cents. The whole thing would cost the chef or caterer $1.38, well within the range to give a 50 percent profit.

"I wanted to get the product out there, so I did the design. I begin with an idea, my imagination. Then I relay my idea to a sketch artist. When the sketches fit my concept, I pass the sketch to a sculpture artist, who returns the design in clay or resin form. Then it is passed on to our mold maker. He makes a casting, which will be used in his mold-making process. The molds are then made out of food-approved material that works well with chocolate. When the chocolate cools and becomes firm, the mold comes off.

Rena had the first molds made at a nearby factory. She had boxes made (24 shells to a box), and then she started marketing. "I made phone calls to four major hotels and talked with the executive chefs, saying 'you have to see this.' I got in to see all four and sold to three of them." It was 1986 and,

CAREER CHECKLIST ✓

You'll like this job if you ...

- Still want to do something, if people say it can't be done

- Have a good eye for design

- Can envision what you want and the steps along the way

- Have enthusiasm and are energetic

- Can do research

- Are confident about your ideas

- Will take a risk

GROUNDBREAKERS

Mrs. Mars

In the late 1890s, Ethel Mars started making chocolates in her tiny kitchen. It was the beginning of the well-known candy empire Mars, Inc. that makes M&Ms, Milky Ways, Three Musketeers, Snickers, and Mars Bars.

In 1911, both Frank and Ethel Mars were making and selling chocolates from their kitchen in Tacoma, Washington. The family's tradition of producing quality confections has been passed down through several generations and is still followed.

Forrest Mars, Sr., who guided the family business for many years, developed a line of gourmet chocolates using the time-honored techniques he had learned from his parents— the best natural ingredients, recipes, and expertise. He named his new venture Ethel M Chocolates after his mother.

with that bear paw shell design that has remained their biggest seller, it was the beginning of Chocolates à la Carte.

A Long Hard Day

Rena's typical day started at 6 a.m. She spent lots of time in her car calling on customers, picking up and delivering chocolate, even helping make the chocolate if the factory making her products got overloaded. "I did everything but the paperwork. My husband, Rick, who was then in the executive search business, had an administrative assistant who luckily was a 'chocoholic.' She did all the billing and bookkeeping and we supplied her with chocolate, of course." (Today, Rick runs the business part of the company as chief executive officer.)

As the business grew, Rena developed more complicated designs. "I went to trade shows and visited different factories; I educated myself." Rena wanted to deliver high-quality chocolate because she knew chocolate lovers didn't want a chocolate mixture; they wanted that real chocolate flavor. "It is difficult to use real chocolate because of the high grade courverture of our designs. That's the challenge I like. I want to do the difficult, what no one else can do." Rena experimented; it was trial and error working with different manufacturers. Now she has her own chocolate machines and furnishes the chocolate to the mold factories. She creates custom designs like corporate logos, chocolate gift boxes, and the elegant chocolate containers for desserts.

Rena's business now employs 200 people and has annual sales of $12 million. Her days are still spent

developing new designs, new product ideas, and meeting people. When she isn't in the office taking calls and working on projects like the latest catalog, she is traveling. She goes to a lot of trade shows and does a lot of charity events, giving back to the industry that has been so good to her.

Daughter of a Retailer

When Rena was growing up in Youngstown, Ohio, she had no idea she would work in the chocolate business. Her dad owned jewelry stores, and she expected to go to college and work in the retail business. "Food was an important part of our life, and I helped make chocolate chip and peanut butter cookies and pies. But I always knew I'd be in business."

Rena went to Emma Willard, a private, all-girls boarding school, in Troy, New York, and was an average student. She was born with a heart defect, and when she was 17, she had to have open heart surgery at the prestigious Johns Hopkins Hospital in Baltimore, Maryland. "I was fortunate to be able to go to them, because that type of surgery was new at that time. They told me I made a strong recovery."

Rena attended Ohio State University in Columbus for two years, taking business courses. But she left college to go to New York City. "I wanted to go into retail and merchandising, and NYC was where the action was." She loved Manhattan and soon was in a program where students attended classes but also got work experience.

During the next few years, Rena worked in various retail jobs, getting merchandising and management experience and loving it. She also began dating her friend Rick—her

> If you have an idea that you really love, develop and expand on it. It's the passion that brings success.

brother is married to Rick's sister. When they got married, Rick convinced her to quit her job so she could travel with him, since his job in the growing high-tech industry meant lots of travel.

Rena spent the next few years as a full-time mom, raising Douglas and Michael. When the boys were ages 3 and 1, Rena and Rick moved to the Los Angeles area, where they live today and run the business.

Next on the agenda may be selling their chocolate covered graham cracker to the public.

Ann Cashion

Ann Cashion

Chef, Co-owner, Cashion's Eat Place, Washington, DC

Major, English Literature

Chef, Restaurant Owner

Cashion's Eat Place

If a restaurant can survive for more than three years in Washington, DC, it's got a fair chance of becoming an institution. So Ann Cashion is feeling good about Cashion's Eat Place, the restaurant she and her partner, John Fulchino, opened May 29, 1995. As the chef and co-owner, Ann spends her time planning the menus, ordering the food, cooking, supervising the staff, and making the thousands of decisions a small business owner needs to make every week.

Ann's cooking has been described by various critics as eclectic country, homey, and delicious. People who visit her restaurant regularly like the friendly and casual atmosphere, the satisfying meals, and the excellent

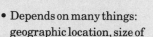

CHEF

- Depends on many things: geographic location, size of restaurant, type of management.

- Entry level, gets liveable wage; higher wages when have management responsibilities like sous chef

- Chef, from $30,000 to $150,000 and higher.

- Extra income from restaurant ownership, teaching, cookbooks, television shows.

service. "My regular customers are interested in what I'm doing and want to take the journey of exploring food with me."

Inspired by the Seasons

Ann uses locally-grown, organic fruits and vegetables and buys meats and other food products from farmers located within a 100-mile radius of her restaurant. She hand writes the menu and changes it daily.

"The seasons are a huge source of my inspiration," she says. "If you want fresh produce, you have to work with what the growers have. For example, you need to realize that there will be lots of tomatoes in July and August, but in February you will want to use more turnips and rutaba-

gas. Today (May) I am working with a large quantity of sorrel we just bought from one of our farmers. It puts pressure on me to come up with creative and interesting dishes using the food that I've purchased." Ann orders every day for the next day's menu, except Sunday, when she tries to use up the food she has ordered during the week.

"Our restaurant has grown in the level of sophistication of the food and the way the operation is run. I now know how to prepare things I couldn't have prepared four years ago."

Ann cooks Wednesday through Sunday morning. The restaurant opens at 5:30 p.m. every day and on Sundays for brunch and dinner. She currently works about 60 hours a week, which is about 40 hours a week less than she worked when she first

Cooks in San
▼ Francisco bakery,
then restaurant

Opens bakeries for
▼ European investors

Cooks for Nora in
▼ Washington, DC

opened the restaurant. "We are closed on Mondays. That was an important decision. It's a guaranteed day when I don't have to be working. Initially I was here every moment we were open. We would start cooking at 10:00 in the morning and serve until 11:00 at night. Then I would have to get cleaned up and do the 'thought' work for the next day. I didn't get home until after midnight six days in a row."

These days Ann tries to take Sunday night off as well as Monday. She lets her staff do the cooking on Tuesday, which gives her a specific day to plan and take care of the administrative details of running a business. Owning a restaurant requires good business skills—a grasp of inventory, of how much it actually costs to produce a dish, of how to schedule the cooking and the staff's work, and of how to find the right people to work with. "Having Sunday nights off gives me a better quality of life outside the restaurant. My Mondays are usually taken up with laundry and errands and eating and sleeping."

"I designed this restaurant with a huge personal involvement in mind. I wanted to push myself as a cook and teach myself a lot of the things I had not had a chance to do before, so it doesn't surprise me that I am working so much. Work is my life. But it's hard to take a block of time off for a vacation. It's expensive to close the restaurant, which is what I did the first year. The second year I wrote a bunch of menus for my staff to prepare while I

was away for a week, and last year I didn't take a vacation. I don't know about this year. One thing you need to realize about the restaurant business is that it is all consuming. I am working when the majority of the world is relaxing, so it's hard to have much of a social life. All my friends, after 22 years in the business, are involved with restaurants. We have a network of people who help and support each other, and we are the ones who know how hard it is and how many hours we have to work."

A Discriminating Palate

As a girl in Mississippi, Ann loved food. She remembers developing a discriminating palate early, because the food served by her mother and her friends' mothers was so good. "Even though it was a lot of the same dishes, they were prepared differently, and I learned to distinguish early which were my favorite ingredients for dishes like potato salad and hush puppies."

Ann's first cooking experience was at a Ramada Inn, where, in high school, she had gotten a job at the reception desk. "I was bored to death and asked the owner, a family friend, if I could work in the kitchen. He was quite surprised because at that time in the South everyone who worked in the kitchen was Black, but he said sure. I was put with a woman and daughter team who did the baking—biscuits, cornbreads, and cakes. They were very good and didn't use recipes. When I tried it at home, I could never make it work. So I thought, well I guess I'm not a good cook. This first job was more about the camaraderie of the kitchen and how the entire staff—cooks, waiters, barmen and barmaids—worked together than it was about learning to cook. The world of the kitchen is a society, and I was fascinated watching people interact with the chef."

From English Studies to Cooking Experience

Ann, influenced by an uncle in New York who taught English literature, went to college at Harvard in Cambridge, Massachusetts. "I thought I would get my Ph.D. in English Literature and then teach like my uncle. I was a very serious student. But, I think it's interesting that I chose to manage one of the house grills and serve students in the evening, after the school kitchens closed. I enjoyed pleasing people with my cooking even then."

Ann got into a Ph.D. program at Stanford University in Palo Alto, California. But she found the heavy emphasis on research isolating, and

CAREER CHECKLIST ✔

You'll like this job if you ...

Consider food an art form

Have a discriminating palate

Can learn quickly

Are willing to work long hours to do what you love

Like to please other people

Love to experiment

Will learn how to run a business

GROUNDBREAKERS

A Beloved Personality, Julia Child

Julia Child, the famous 6 foot 2 inch, older woman with the enthusiastic manner and distinctive voice, became well known for doing one of the first successful cooking shows on television (1963-1966) and for writing *Mastering the Art of French Cooking*.

Born in 1912, Julia grew up in California. According to her biographer, she was a high-spirited girl and the center of every prank and party during her years at Smith College. Julia got a job with the OSS (Office of Strategic Services in the Secret Intelligence branch of the U.S. government). During World War II, she was in India and China, where she met her future husband, Paul Child, who introduced her to fine French food.

She began her culinary training at age 37 at the Cordon Bleu in France. She invested 10 years of learning and experimenting, then in 1961, wrote her classic book on French cooking. Since then she has written many books. Noel Riley Fitch wrote *Appetite for Life*, her biography.

she didn't like specializing in one area exclusively, even though she was studying some of the greatest poets of the English language. "Even with my cooking, I'm more of a generalist than a specialist. What attracted me about the Ph.D. program was teaching, but the things you had to go through to get to that point were just too excruciating."

One semester she went to Italy, where Stanford had a campus. "I did not do any work. I ended up visiting all the restaurants in Florence and thinking a lot about food."

When she returned to the United States, Ann stuck it out at Stanford for one more year and wondered whether she could have a career as a chef. At that time (the late 1970s) San Francisco was the center of a new American cuisine—simply prepared food using organically grown, fresh, and high-quality ingredients. This environment had a huge influence on Ann, encouraging her to leave school and get her first real cooking job at a bakery in San Francisco, run by a Swiss woman who had married a French man.

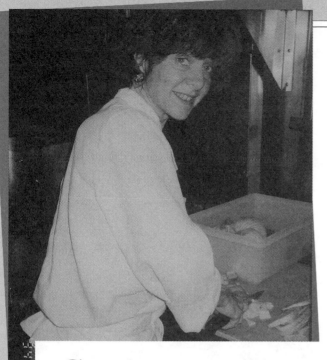

the grill, hand-rolled dough for the pastas, pure ingredients, and simple preparation. It reinforced her beliefs about preparing food. "This was the closest I ever came to a culinary school. I stayed as long as I could—six months—but I was paying for my apartment in San Francisco at the same time and it was expensive. They only paid me a little bit at the restaurant. After

> Getting positive feedback from customers is a big part of what I love about the work. It juices me up to hear a customer say they've had 'such a great meal, this is so delicious.'

Next, Ann decided she wanted to learn to cook like the Italians. She arranged an apprenticeship near Florence at a Tuscan restaurant she had visited frequently. She learned Tuscan cooking—only wood fires for

all, I was the one who wanted to learn, and I didn't bring anything to the party—there was nothing I could teach them."

Back in San Francisco, Ann couldn't find a job using her Tuscan cooking skills. She cooked in a small restaurant where the food was good, but learned little except how to be an American commercial cook. Then Ann joined a group of Europeans who wanted to open shops with high-quality, mass-produced French breads and pastries. They sent her to France to learn high-tech ways to freeze bakery products and Ann opened two stores for them. Then she moved to Washington, DC, because the person she was dating had taken a job there.

Even in San Francisco, Ann had heard about Restaurant Nora, which in the early 1980s had gained a reputation for its well-prepared food. Everything was made from organic ingredients. Ann ate there to make sure she liked it, asked Nora for a job, and was hired. Ann learned a lot about the local growers who supplied the fresh food at Nora's.

After spending a couple of years with Nora, Ann was crazy with the desire to open her own restaurant. She took a year off to plan her own place. Her first challenges were to find a location and to raise the money to launch her restaurant. But raising the money turned out to be an impossibility. "It was the marketplace

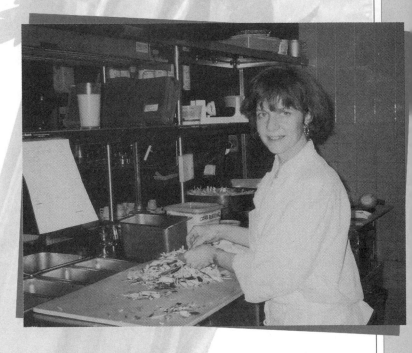

reflecting the fact that I didn't have enough experience to be an owner/chef yet." (To open her own restaurant today, Ann would need between $250,000 and $800,000.)

The Tex-Mex Experience

Ann worked part-time as a bartender while she was doing the research on her restaurant. Her savings were almost gone when she met Rob Wilder, who wanted to open a Tex-Mex restaurant in Washington with authentic southwestern U.S. food. Initially, Ann was hired as the menu consultant—the person who would decide what the restaurant would serve. Because she knew nothing about this type of food, she spent some months in Austin, Texas, and Santa Fe, New Mexico, tasting the dishes local people thought were the best. Gradually, she formed her own ideas of how to make the concept of Tex-Mex food work in Washington, DC. She had fallen in love with the food. She told Rob that she would cook for him in his new restaurant, The Austin Grill.

Here Ann gained valuable experience in every aspect of running a restaurant—from hiring and training the staff, to ordering the food, to making sure there was a healthy profit. She also cooked every day. She stayed with Rob for eight years, during which they opened another Austin Grill in Alexandria, Virginia, and a Spanish restaurant called Jaleo in DC. At Austin Grill, Ann met and worked with her current business partner, John. By this time she was pretty comfortable running Austin Grill, but he pushed her to open her own place.

"He was right. Having my own restaurant, I'm as happy as I've ever been. But the anxiety level is higher sometimes too. So many people depend on me."

Ann's latest challenge is to keep the high quality in her own restaurant while she and her partner open a simple, but good seafood place. "We want to have a consistent product that is good, so that customers know what to expect. It will be very different from Cashion's, where every day is a new experience."

Judy G. Koyama

Judy Gee Koyama

Owner, East West Specialty Sauces, Inc., Denver, CO

Major in Business Administration

Specialty Foods Manufacturer

Savory and Saucy

Judy Gee Koyama makes sauce about three or four times a week. Judy is the creator and owner of East West Specialty Sauces. Her company manufactures seven different oriental sauces that are sold in grocery stores all over Colorado and in parts of Texas, Nebraska, Wyoming, and California. Judy makes Sweet and Spicy Ginger Teriyaki Sauces, Low Fat Sweet and Spicy Ginger Teriyaki Sauces, Classic Sweet and Sour and Tropical Lemon Dipping and Glazing Sauces, and Tangy Mandarin Barbecue Sauce.

On the day before sauce making at her factory in Denver, Colorado, she prepares all the ingredients that will be needed for the cooking and bottle

ENTREPRENEUR EARNINGS

People who start their own business may not earn any salary in the beginning. They invest their own money in the business, they get more money through loans or venture capital, and until they make a profit or "go public" by selling stock, they probably pay themselves a small salary and put profits back into the business to help it grow. Sometimes when they sell the business, they sign a contract that pays them executive compensation to stay and manage the company.

JUDY'S CAREER PATH

Works in The
▼ Jade Palace

Graduates college,
▼ gets teaching
certificate

Marries Keith
▼

filling. She positions soy sauce, fresh garlic and ginger, spices, and saki wine so they can easily be added to the mixture, which will be cooked in big vats. She arranges the bottles, labels, decorative foil, and caps so that bottles can be filled and labels and foil can be placed by hand. Caps are put

workers include her mother and father, her sister (sometimes), and aunts and uncles. "These people want to work a little, not much, and to have the social interaction that they get from a day of sauce making," Judy says. "I give them lunch. We celebrate a little at the end of our filling ses-

In a small business, you may have to do everything for awhile—produce the food, make the sales, market the product.

on by a capping machine. "We've been adding equipment so that we are semi-automated now," Judy says. "We used to do everything by hand."

On sauce making days, several relatives—most of them over the age of 65—show up to help with the fill. The

sions by catching up on news of what everybody is doing. The older people look forward to days when we fill. For me, it's an advantage because I only pay them for the hours they work; they aren't full-time employees and so we don't have to do all the other

Teaches in high
school

Has triplets

Begins East West
Specialty Sauces

things you have to do with full-time employees."

Judy makes enough sauce to fulfill the orders from her distributors (companies that sell to the grocery stores), and some extra, so that she can immediately fulfill any new sales. "It takes the same amount of time to clean up no matter how long you fill, so it's more efficient to spend as much of a day filling as possible," she says. On

days when Judy isn't cooking and supervising the fill, she is busy ordering supplies for the business, making sales calls or taking orders from stores and distributors, doing record keeping and accounting, and planning marketing strategies so she can get her sauces sold in more stores.

In The Stores

On the weekends, she and her husband Keith, a high school assistant principal, are usually at supermarkets passing out samples. "Many companies hire demonstration firms to do this," Judy says. "But we like to do it ourselves because we know how important it is to get good exposure in a new store. On the weekends, the stores are the most

JUDY'S CAREER PATH

Opens office building
▼ cafeteria

Runs East West
▼ Specialty Sauces
full-time

crowded, so it's the best time to sell the sauces. The late afternoon is the very best time, because people are trying to decide what to have for dinner and they are hungry.

"We go to the supermarket early in the morning to get a good spot. I take chicken breasts and a stainless grill to cook on. We let the customers choose the sauce they would like to try. At some stores, there are lots of hungry college kids who 'know the routine.' They return again and again. But you can't be rude to them. Only the store manager can ever say no to a customer in a grocery store. So you have to learn to handle these things diplomatically, or the store won't do business with you."

Judy's business is very small in comparison to her competitors, large, nationally-known companies that

sell in just about every grocery store. She thinks it's important to hit all the stores where her sauces are on the shelves. So far, this strategy has paid off. In the Colorado area, where the product has been in the stores the longest, it is number four in oriental sauces, just behind the national brands. Judy has decided to spend money making trips to other areas of the country—California and Texas, where her product has recently been introduced—and setting up sample tables in stores, rather than spending money on advertisements in newspapers and magazines. "In this business they track everything—all sales—using the Universal Product Code that appears on every product. Each store knows how every product is doing in the store. If your product doesn't sell, the store buyer can kick it off the shelves. It's so hard to get into a store that once we are there, we want to be sure we stay there."

Food a Big Part of Life

Judy grew up in the food business. Her parents, the Gees, were immigrants from Mainland China. They ran kitchens for bar owners, and in Judy's senior year of high school, opened their own Chinese restaurant in Denver called The Jade Palace. For nearly 30 years, Judy played a big part in running it. She worked there on weekends while she was in college. After she married, she worked at the restaurant, doing part of the cooking, ordering the supplies, and helping to keep the books.

One day, a good customer asked Judy to make some sweet Teriyaki sauce for a party she was giving on July 4th, a day the restaurant was closed. The gesture of having sauce to take home was so appreciated that making sauce for good customers became a tradition. Judy didn't charge

CAREER CHECKLIST ✓

You'll like this job if you ...

- Have an entrepreneurial spirit

- Would like to build something and see the results

- Have a strong feel for what people want in food products

- Will learn about business principles, like profit and loss, inventory, and sales

- Will work long hours

- Can get along with many different types of people

GROUNDBREAKERS

Original Ideas for Fine Food

Through research and experimentation, Lucille Bishop Smith (an African American resident of Fort Worth, Texas) developed and published many original ideas on the culinary arts. She reportedly developed the first hot roll mix in the United States and set up the first Commercial Foods and Technology Department at the college level with an apprenticeship training program at Prairie View A & M College. She published a cookbook, *Lucille's Treasure Chest of Fine Foods*, and at age 82, founded and became president of her family corporation, Lucille B. Smith's Fine Foods, Inc.

these customers any money. Eventually, someone suggested she try to sell the sauces she made. She thought about it and decided to give it a try.

Judy had a lot to learn about making a food product saleable in stores. The first challenge was to create a sauce that would have a shelf life (not spoil over time). The sauces Judy made for The Jade Palace were used right away in cooking, but the bottled sauce had to maintain its flavor and intensity if it was stored for a long time. Judy turned to the state agriculture office for advice and also got some help from a local university. The agriculture office and the university food experts helped her choose ingredients that resulted in a proper acid balance for long storage.

Next, Judy had to learn about labeling and the regulations of the U.S. Food and Drug Administration. Any food product sold in the United States must be labeled properly with nutritional facts and tested for safety by the FDA. The items must be manufactured in a healthy and sanitary facility according to government regulations. But these were easy challenges in comparison to getting her products into the right distribution channels so that many people could see and buy them.

"I was incredibly lucky," Judy says.

decides to work with your product, he will help you to place it in many different stores. It's the distributor's job to go to the stores, see what is selling, and be sure product is available and shelves get stocked.

My girls can have this business some day if they want it. It's hard to raise a family and have a full-time job. This would allow them a little flexibility and control in their lives.

"Usually people like me, who are making one food product, never get to see a buyer for a store. But by sheer persistence, I met a really nice buyer from Safeway, a chain of grocery stores, and he agreed to taste it. He liked it, and he gave me lots of good advice about how to get started."

The buyer recommended a reputable distributor who agreed to handle the products. Once a distributor

Teriyaki Sauce First

Even though Judy was born in China (she came to this country when she was 5 years old) and has two Chinese parents, her first sauce for sale in a bottle was a Japanese sauce, Teriyaki. Judy had a roommate in college who served her a dish made with Teriyaki sauce. Judy sort of liked it. She fiddled with the basic ingredients until she got it exactly the way she wanted it and then served it to family and friends. They raved about it.

Serving Teriyaki in her home wasn't as strange for a Chinese woman as it might seem, especially since she is married to a man of Japanese descent. Judy's husband, Keith Koyama, grew up in Hawaii, the son of two Japanese Americans. Judy met Keith at college and the couple married the year they graduated. Both were teachers, and they found teaching jobs in Nebraska. But when Judy's younger brother, Tony, got very sick, Judy's parents needed her to help out at the restaurant. Judy and Keith returned to Denver, where Keith found a teaching job. In 1976, Judy gave birth to triplets—Heather,

Jasmine, and Kelly. Working at The Jade Palace was a convenient job. She could be home with the girls when

needed and could work at the restaurant when Keith was home with the kids. Keith also worked at the restaurants on weekends.

She Opens A Cafeteria

Judy began experimenting with sauces in 1992. By 1994, she was placed in stores in the Denver area.

days in the cafeteria and nights making sauces. By this time, she had found a location for her sauce factory at the edge of town and had begun investing in some equipment. After three years of running the cafeteria and saving some money to put into her sauce business, she quit to devote full-time to making and selling sauces.

In 1998, one of the biggest distribu-

The most important thing for a small business person like me is persistence. You just have to keep knocking on doors until you get noticed. You can't give up.

At this time, the triplets were grown up and in college, and Judy felt it was time to do something different. Judy knew the owner of an office building who wanted someone to operate a cafeteria on the premises. He would not charge her for the space and she could keep the profits. She worked

tors in California placed her in some California grocery stores. A competitor was selling her product, and the distributors' grocery chain wanted to offer it too. Judy also broke into a market in Texas her first year working full-time in her sauce business.

Julie Simonson

Julie Simonson

Manager, Kraft Foods Inc., Glenview, Illinois

Major in Food Science, Ph.D. Food Science, University of Minnesota

Food Scientist

Her Challenge is New and Improved Foods

Julie Simonson develops new and better ways to process food at Kraft Foods. She leads a team of 13 food scientists and engineers who conduct research to identify and develop new technologies. The group identifies and tests technologies that can be used in the development of new products or that will save money in the manufacture of food products.

Julie and her team explore all types of technologies for all the areas of the company—cheeses, meats, salad dressings, cereals, beverages, desserts, dinners, and other Kraft Foods products. They must keep up with the latest research in food processing technologies and market trends. What are consumers buying?

FOOD SCIENTIST

- Average salary ranges from $55,000 to $70,000
- Scientists with higher degrees and experience may earn more.

Source: Encyclopedia of Careers and Vocational Guidance

JULIE'S CAREER PATH

Active in 4-H, experiments with muffins

Gets $10,000 scholarship to college

Has internships with food companies

What types of products not yet on the market would consumers buy? What types of technologies are other food companies using? For example, food scientists are discovering new ways to make food more convenient to use or tastier. Food scientists also work on how to add ingredients to foods to make them healthier, such as adding calcium to cereal or orange juice.

Julie is responsible for setting the strategy for her team of food scientists and engineers. She helps the group decide what technologies to concentrate on and makes sure that the research is going in the right direction. Members of Julie's team might experiment with processed cheese to see how the cheese performs with a new ingredient. The researchers would have to test how the ingredient affected the flavor, the texture, and the "meltabili-ty" of the cheese. If the cheese didn't melt right, researchers would need to look at its properties to determine the problem and find a way to alter the ingredients so that the cheese melted correctly.

One-on-one Meetings

On a typical day, Julie gets to the office around 7:30 a.m., checks her voice mail and her email, writes memos, and does paperwork She holds her meetings with members of her team during the "core" business hours. (Many companies with flexible hours ask their employees to work certain core hours and then the employees can work their additional hours later or earlier in the day, depending on what they like.) From 9:00 a.m. until 4:00 p.m., her day is filled with various meetings. At the

Skips master's,
▼ gets Ph.D.

Ph.D

Marries Dave, lands
▼ job at Kraft as
research scientist

Has daughter
▼ Emily

end of the day, she makes some phone calls and catches up on more paperwork, leaving for home by about 6:00 p.m. each evening.

Julie meets with each member of the team individually at least once every two weeks to find out how the research project is going and to make suggestions to help the scientist solve problems. She helps them get the information they need from other departments within the company or from other researchers.

Another of Julie's responsibilities is to make sure that the food scientists and engineers who work for her have opportunities to take classes that will help them gain more knowledge and develop the expertise they need to move into higher level positions within the company. Julie also makes sure

each of them has a mentor (a manager or high-level scientist or engineer to provide advice about how to operate within the company).

Julie leads the team that conducts the preliminary research on the new technologies. Then her group transfers

Gets promoted, has
daughter Kari

Gets promoted to research
section manager of future
technologies

the technology to a particular Kraft category (such as salad dressings) for more research, and ultimately for use in products sold on the market.

"The whole challenge for a food company is that there are so many items on the grocery shelves. Consumers have many alternatives, so we want to make sure the product is as good as it can be. We have to compete with all of their choices. Launching a new product takes lots of money for advertising—coupons in newspapers and magazines, television ads, samples at the stores."

Fat Free and Full of Flavor

Julie started her career at Kraft, as a research scientist in pourable salad dressings. She worked on fat free

dressings just after they were first developed, experimenting with formulas that could improve the taste and texture. Then Julie's boss told her to work on a new flavor of ranch dressing, Caesar Ranch, that would provide some variety from the buttermilk and plain ranch dressings then on the market. She started doing some experimentation in the pilot plant and

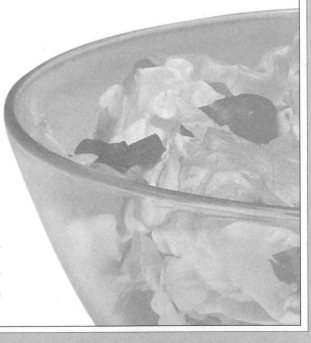

came up with a flavor that worked. Then there were consumer tests to make sure people really liked it. Finally, it went to market "It was so neat to go to the grocery store and see people putting that dressing in their shopping carts," Julie says.

After a few years, Julie was promoted to senior research scientist. She led a team working on a line of herb dressings that were later sold in supermarkets. In this job, she worked with Kraft people across the whole company—marketing, research, finance, and manufacturing. She and a colleague founded a "Pourables Roundtable," a way for those who worked in plant operations to get together and talk with the research scientists who developed the new technologies for pourable salad dressings.

Because Julie was so good at managing—she had leadership skills and knew how to influence people and to negotiate effectively—she got another promotion to the dinners category, where she was responsible for the macaroni and cheese dinners and the refrigerated pasta and sauce busi-

CAREER CHECKLIST ✓

You'll like this job if you ...

- Are good in science and like school

- Like to cook

- Have excellent communication skills, can speak well and influence people

- Like to solve problems

- Are good in math

- Can work with people of all different ages, races, and outlooks

- Want to work for a big company with plenty of room for advancement

GROUNDBREAKERS

Beginnings of Home Economics

Ellen Swallow Richards (1842-1911) was a chemist, ecologist, and home economist. She was the first woman student at Massachusetts Institute of Technology (MIT). She convinced MIT to establish the Woman's Laboratory, where she taught chemical analysis, industrial chemistry, and biology from 1876 to 1883, when the school began accepting women as regular students. In 1884 she was formally made instructor of sanitary chemistry. She studied and taught sanitary engineering, and with her emphasis on the interplay between the physical, biological and social, she is regarded as the founder of ecology, which intertwined consumer and environmental concerns. These later split apart as the environmental branch became male dominated and the consumer branch, female dominated. In 1889, Richards began a series of summer conferences on making home care easier and cooking nutritious meals, calling it home economics. She helped found the American Home Economics Association.

ness. After one and one half years in that position, Julie was promoted to her current position as section manager, in charge of finding new technologies Kraft can use in the future.

Mom's 4-H Club

Julie credits her mom with having given her an interest in food by encouraging her to be in 4-H. Julie's mom was a stay-at-home mom. She started a 4-H club in their home town in Iowa when Julie was just a baby. By the time Julie was 9, she was in the club and doing all sorts of projects—clothing, home improvement, and food and nutrition.

Julie liked the food projects the best. She loved experimenting with food. She took many of her experiments to 4-H events and county and state fairs. For example, she displayed an experiment in which she had not fully kneaded dough. When she was in high school, she did a semester-long independent study in which she substituted high fructose corn syrup for sugar in muffins. Her mom took her to the

University of Iowa and Iowa State University to study the literature on how to do this type of experiment. She visited food science classes at the universities to understand how to set up a sensory study on muffins and how to best measure the muffins' texture. She recruited women from her church to be on a sensory panel to taste the muffins. They would come to her house once a

But the decision of what to study in college wasn't easy because Julie had another love—music. She had started playing the bassoon in the 7th grade. She thought about a career as a bassoonist, and up to the time she was applying to colleges, she didn't know which major—food science or music—she wanted to pursue. But a $10,000 scholarship to Iowa State University

> I had two internships—one with Nestle and one with Nabisco—and they were both wonderful experiences. They gave me more of a sense of what the food processing world is like and helped me get my job at Kraft.

month and taste her latest recipe. "It was about this time that I discovered that I really loved food science and began to consider it as a possible career. I was in awe of those college students who were studying food science."

for outstanding incoming freshman students decided her course of study. She got that scholarship and majored in food science.

But Julie didn't give up her music. She continued to play in the university orchestra and in small groups. She still plays in a community orchestra and plays handbells in a church handbell choir. "I'm at orchestra practice every Monday night. I love to practice with the orchestra. It's always been a total diversion from the scientific side of my brain. The music allows me to have a different kind of freedom. It's totally different than the other things I do."

When she got her undergraduate degree in food science, Julie started looking for a job. But with only a bachelor's degree, she couldn't find jobs that interested her. So she applied for and got a teaching and research assistantship at the University of Minnesota under Dr. Howard Morris, a food science professor. Dr. Morris helped Julie to pursue her Ph.D. in food science without going through the master's program. With his encouragement and help, she got special permission to work on a Ph.D., which she earned in three and one half years, instead of the five years usually necessary for a doctorate. "Dr. Morris was interested in students getting the knowledge they needed and then going to work in the real world." Julie's assistantship paid for her tuition and left enough money to rent a small apartment in St. Paul.

Her First Job

In physical chemistry at graduate school, Julie met Dave, now her husband. The two were friends for a cou-

At college, I had to take food chemistry, physical chemistry, rheology (the study of fluid flow), physics, chemistry, fluid mechanics, food microbiology, statistics—specifically experimental design—and processing courses (milk processing and cheese making courses).

ple of years and then started dating. When Julie graduated with her doctorate, they married. Julie started working for Kraft, and the couple moved to the Chicago suburbs. Dave found a job with a food company, where he worked for six years as a quality supervisor on the second shift—3:00 p.m. to 1:00 a.m. When the couple's first child, Emily, was born, Dave took care of her during the day and Julie took care of her at night. They were only together on the weekends.

But after their second child, Kari, was born, Julie and Dave decided that one of them needed to stay home with the girls full-time. Because Julie loved her job and Dave's job was just a job to him, he decided to stay home. "We figured out you can make it on one salary if you cut out some things—not eating out so much, not having to pay for day care, and saving on gas. Our plans are to do this as long as we can, because we feel it is important for the girls to have someone at home."

Mary Maczko

Mary Maczko

Sergeant First Class, S-4, Group Food Service Supervisor,
64th Corps Support Group, U.S. Army, Fort Hood, TX

Military
Food
Service

Soldiers' First Class Cook

Mary Maczko joined the U.S. Army as a cook. The thing she likes best about her job is the satisfaction of soldiers telling her that the food is great. Mary has cooked for soldiers and she has supervised cooks. She's done leadership training, managed large dining rooms, and been in charge of moving supplies during the Gulf War in Saudi Arabia. She's even served as an Equal Opportunity Advisor to soldiers in Korea and Germany. Now she is the first sergeant for the first and only company of cooks at Fort Hood, Texas. "This isn't an easy career for a woman, so you have to really love it."

Mary has been in the Army for 16 years. After basic training, she took

U.S. MILITARY

- Persons in the U.S. armed services get housing and meals as part of their pay.
- Private First Class $1,200 per month
- Sergeant, experienced $2,900 per month

MARY'S CAREER PATH

Studies medical
science in
college

Supports 2 children,
works in pants
factory

Joins Army
as cook

food service training and then was assigned to Fort Lewis, Washington, for her first tour of duty. "The first thing they did was to put me into the field with an aviation unit in Yakima. I had only been in the area three days. I cooked in a tent with gas-operated burners. I set up the tent with field stoves, tables, and pallets to store food. We had about 12 cooks for the battalion, and there were three women. I learned a lot there. I hadn't known how to bake before I went into the Army. In the field I learned how to make good biscuits. When you are in the field, the soldiers have to eat what you prepare because there is nowhere else to go. They will tell you if the food really sucks, so you want to learn quickly how to cook well."

Back at Fort Lewis garrison, Mary cooked for aviators and rangers (special combat soldiers). "That's where I learned how to operate a grill. These guys wanted nothing but double cheeseburgers and omelets with everything on them."

As a private first class, she worked as a clerk to a food service sergeant. He was a proficient cook and showed her how to survive in the field. She worked with another sergeant who

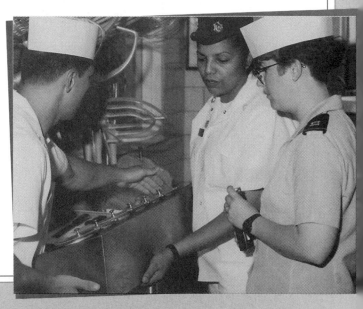

Works in
▼ Washington state,
Germany

Manages dining facility
▼ at Fort Campbell

Goes to Gulf War in
▼ Saudi Arabia

knew everything about administration and showed her how to run a dining facility. "This was actually lucky for me. I learned all the administrative stuff early on in my career, although at the time I thought I should have been cooking instead." At Fort Lewis, Mary received her first Army promotion, to specialist. Then the Army sent her to Germany.

In Germany, It was Gravy

When she was moved to a position as cook, she worked with a lot of German civilians who had been hired to cook on the base. "Even though I knew how to make biscuits and had been a shift leader, I didn't know how to make gravy. You have a recipe card, but if you haven't made it be-

fore, chances are you are going to burn it. Fortunately, German cooks have to go to school for a long time before they can work as a cook. They have to learn to make more than 100 different gravies, so I learned from them how to do it."

One thing made Mary unhappy. The Army wouldn't send her to the field in Germany. Most women who were cooks didn't want to go, but Mary did. For one thing, you got extra money for temporary duty in the field. Also, if you learned how to use the field equipment and cook well there, you would have more options for career moves later on.

Asking Questions, Getting Answers

Mary is the type of person who does not like to take "no" for an answer.

"Some people say I'm cocky, but I'm just confident of the things I can do." She finally got to go to field exercises and got an award for managing the field kitchen.

Mary had already won an award for "cook of the quarter," and she knew she was qualified to be a sergeant. When she asked her colonel why she hadn't gotten board approval, she found out the soldier in charge of forwarding her paperwork to the board lost her paperwork!

Mary also wanted to know why cooks who won awards didn't get to go to East Berlin, like the Military Police (MPs) did. She was in a unit of MPs and they were given a week's trip to East Berlin when they won awards. Her colonel admitted she was right. He arranged for her to go to East Berlin for winning cook of the quarter,

and he sent her to the promotion board, paperwork or no paperwork. The week before she approached the board for promotion approval, she got her trip to East Berlin. Then she got her board approval. (The board looks at skills and knowledge, training and schooling, physical fitness, and weapons qualifications when determining who is promotable. The competition is tough, because only so many soldiers can be promoted during the course of a year.)

The approval from the board meant that Mary could finally get promoted to sergeant. This was important, because her rank now allowed her to get housing for dependents on the base, and that meant her children could move to Germany and live with her. Mary had married young and had two children. She and her husband had divorced and the children had been living with her parents. She spent three and one half years in Germany, and she knocked herself out trying to be a good mom and an Army cook.

The Only Female Instructor

For Mary's next career move, she got a job as a leadership development instructor, which consisted of teaching soldiers at Fort Campbell, Kentucky, how to prepare for being a sergeant. She taught soldiers map reading and navigation for two years and was the first female inducted into the Hall of Excellence as instructor of the month. In fact, Mary was the only female instructor. She could not use the showers for the instructors, who were all men, and instead used the showers for the students, because there were women students. Mary thought her higher rank relieved her of showering with the students, so she barged into the instructors' showers one day and said she was

CAREER CHECKLIST ✔

You'll like this job if you ...

- Aren't afraid to speak up for yourself

- Can stand up to authority but also take orders

- Are good at managing projects

- Like to cook or can learn quickly

- Know how to network with others to get what you need

- Won't mind working with lots of men

- Have pride in yourself and your country

GROUNDBREAKERS

Fannie Farmer

Fannie Merritt Farmer (1857-1915) was an American cook and educator in Boston. When she was 40 years old, she published the *Boston Cooking School Cook Book*, which in later editions became the *Fannie Farmer Cookbook*. Her methods earned her the nickname "Mother of Level Measurement." She introduced precise measurements and instructions. In 1902 she founded Miss Farmer's School of Cookery, which offered courses on nutrition for nursing mothers and nutrition for children. She also was an advisor to Harvard Medical School on diets. In 1904 she published *Food and Cooking for the Sick and Convalescent*.

going to begin showering there. The men complained, but when she started taking off her clothes, they got out of her way. Then they complained to the major, who merely said it looked like she knew how to take care of herself.

"In the military, contrary to the civilian sector, when we have our little gender-bender fights, we tend to win, because the military really does try to be equal opportunity. I grew up with four brothers, three of them who later became marines, and I knew what I had to do to make my way."

Food for Gulf War Soldiers

From leadership development instructor, Mary became assistant dining facility manager at a general's mess. She helped cater lawn parties for generals and worked in the dining facility. Then the war in the Gulf broke out, and Mary's unit (101st Airborne Division) was sent to Saudi Arabia. She stayed behind a short time to turn the cooking equipment over to the civilian cooks and make sure that the cooks who were being deployed to Saudi were good enough for the soldiers at war. "If soldiers don't have good food, they lose all motivation." She arranged for her children to stay with their grandparents as she prepared to go to Saudi Arabia.

In Saudi Arabia, the food service people undertook four missions—to support the troops at the front, in the middle, in the rear, and the general's mess. Mary's job in Saudi Arabia was to make sure that the food moved forward on schedule. She also had to make sure the cooks had the right equipment to do their jobs and the cooking tents were set up properly as the Army moved forward. She was also responsible for communications about other supplies, such as boots for the soldiers.

"It was stressful in Saudi Arabia. Some of my friends died, some people had nervous breakdowns, and if you went out on a mission to bring back food, there was always the chance you would be the victim of a bomb or ground fire. But you just do what you have to do."

After nine months in Saudi Arabia, Mary returned to Fort Campbell and married Matt, a man she had met in the Gulf War. He too was a cook. They were always in friendly competition for awards for the dining facilities after that. Mary managed one dining facility and Matt managed another. They competed against each other in many culinary arts competitions too, including ice carvings, decorated cakes, and other types of fancy food displays. About this time, Mary got promoted to sergeant first class, rank-

ing 33rd out of about 1,800 cooks who were up for that promotion nationwide.

Mary was getting bored, because she had done just about everything in food service, when her mentor, a female sergeant major, challenged her to take the worst dining facility on the base and turn it around. When Mary went to interview with the colonel in charge of free, where before soldiers had to pay for it. "I could do it because I had learned marketing skills." Mary's facility was so successful that soldiers from other dining facilities started eating there and that created a problem—not enough food to meet the demand. She worked it out, though. She fed her soldiers first, and then let the others eat there if there was enough food.

What I like best is the satisfaction you get seeing the soldiers happy with what they are eating.

that facility, she took a list of things she would need in order to make the dining facility good. "No one ever comes to me with a list of demands," the colonel said. But Mary explained that these were the things she would need to succeed—close the facility down for cleaning, order new equipment, create a schedule that would allow the cooks some time off during the weekends, change the menu to food the soldiers liked. The colonel agreed to her requests and she revamped the entire facility, offering some food that was

When her husband retired from the Army and her kids had graduated from high school, Mary wanted to travel more. Her husband, who got a job driving a truck after he retired from the Army, decided to stay at Fort Campbell. Mary didn't have enough service years to retire. She wanted to do what was best for her career, so she went overseas. She got a job as Equal Opportunity Advisor, addressing the complaints of soldiers who felt they were being treated unfairly because of their gender or their race. She spent one and one-half years in Korea and one year in Germany.

After her tours of duty overseas, she got assigned to Fort Hood, where she now works, as a food service supervisor. Her current job involves figuring out how to provide the best food for the soldiers at dining facilities and helping the facilities to compete with all the fast food places now common on Army bases. She is responsible for a company of cooks at Fort Hood.

A New Yorker and Puerto Rican

Mary grew up in Brooklyn, New York, the daughter of Puerto Rican parents. She lived in a neighborhood filled with people from different parts of the world. In high school she went to an international school for fashion in New York. She was interested in modeling and fashion design. After high school she started college, studying medical science on a scholarship she earned with her 4.0 grade point average. But she lost her scholarship be-

cause she got tired of school and took time off. She got married to a man she met at a summer camp where she was teaching ecology. The marriage didn't last long, and Mary and her two young children returned to New York. Mary's daughter is now a nurses' assistant in the Air Force and her son, who served in the U.S. Navy, now sells computers.

Mary worked at a pants factory as a secretary until she decided to enter the Army at the age of 29. "I wanted my kids to experience the international life. And I wanted to earn a better living for my kids."

Debra Stark

Debra Stark

Owner, Debra's Natural Gourmet, Concord, MA;
Creator of Stark Sisters Granola

Major in Russian Studies

Health Food
Store Owner

Eat Well, Be Happy

Eat well, be happy is the philosophy by which Debra Stark runs her business. Debra is the owner of Debra's Natural Gourmet in Concord, Massachusetts. With her sister-in-law, Mary, Debra also manufactures Stark Sisters Granola, sold in grocery and specialty stores throughout the country in flavors like Nutty Maple Molasses and Maple Almond.

Debra's store in Concord employs 26 people. It is one of the best stocked, natural food stores in the country. If a customer asks for something Debra doesn't carry, and it's a product she believes is good for you, she'll order it. The store also sells such cooked dishes as vegetarian lasagna, oriental green beans with sesame seeds, and pumpkin maple cake—all made from recipes Debra has invented or perfect-

ENTREPRENEUR EARNINGS

People who start their own business may not earn any salary in the beginning. They invest their own money in the business, they get more money through loans or venture capital, and, until they make a profit or "go public" by selling stock, they probably pay themselves a small salary and put profits back into the business to help it grow. Sometimes when they sell the business, they sign a contract that pays them executive compensation to stay and manage the company.

ed. The kitchen, on the premises, is open seven days a week so that customers who don't feel like cooking can pick up cooked food that is nutritious and healthy. There is always something new and intriguing to try.

Besides running the store, Debra and Mary manufacture, market, and sell

When Debra started the gourmet store in 1987, she worked seven days a week, 12 hours every day. She didn't take a salary and she and her then 14-year old son, Adam, ate the leftovers that nobody bought from the store's kitchen.

Debra started Debra's Natural

We could lower our nation's health care costs tremendously if we just learned to eat right.

Stark Sisters Granola, a gourmet cereal with no preservatives. It is made of organic grains, roasted until they are crunchy. Stark Sisters Granola was named one of the 10 best holiday food gifts by *The New York Times* newspaper and recognized as a good holiday gift by *Bon Appetite* magazine.

Gourmet using all her savings. Her mother, father, and brothers chipped in and helped, too, so Debra could open the store. Within two years, she was able to pay them back the money they had loaned her. Soon she was experiencing rapid growth in sales and expanded the number and types of products she

Teaches in Israel

Marries

Son, Adam, is born

offered, providing her customers with even more variety.

Mother was a Big Influence

Debra grew up in Orlando, Florida. Her mother, who was somewhat of a free thinker, had an interest in natural foods. When Debra was a girl, there were always crates of organic produce and raw milk around the house. Debra's mother was one of the original subscribers to *Prevention* magazine, which is well-respected for information about natural foods as preventive medicine and remedies for illnesses. Debra's mother got interested in natural foods when her sister became very ill. The doctor said she wouldn't live long. But Debra's aunt prolonged her life by making sure she got proper nutrition. She "converted" the whole family.

"My mother had learned that nutrition could play a big role in health. She made us read labels and learn the ingredients on products sold in grocery stores. But she didn't forbid my brother and me from eating the way we wanted to. I remember trading the wonderful lunches she made for white bread sandwiches at school. That was before I knew better. Later I became convinced of the power of eating well."

lege, Debra landed a job in Israel teaching English in a junior high school. She is Jewish, and in the back of her mind she wanted to meet a Jewish man. In Israel she met and married her husband, Boaz, an

If you believe in something and are passionate about it, you have to act on it.

After graduating from high school, Debra went to college in New York City. She lived in Greenwich Village, which was famous at that time for its radical notions and emphasis on the nontraditional. She found a job in a natural food store there while studying Russian at Washington Square College. After she graduated from col-

Israeli student. They returned to the United States and her husband began studying for his Ph.D. in industrial psychology at the University of Michigan.

Debra helped put her husband through school by waitressing, teaching piano, and doing office work. The couple served as the house parents at

a home for retarded adults in Detroit. It was a fascinating and rewarding experience. Debra loved teaching things to her house mates.

In 1975, Adam was born. Debra and her husband had been drifting further and further apart, and in 1978 she decided to strike out on her own. She and her son moved to Concord, Massachusetts, near Debra's parents. For some years she worked "9 to 5" jobs (like legal secretary and office manager) that would allow her to be there for her son when he came home from school.

But Debra had always loved food—shopping for it, preparing it, and arranging it—a love she inherited from her mother. She didn't like the natural foods stores that existed in the area and thought the community could use a natural foods store within walking distance of the center of her town.

Getting the store started was difficult at first. Even though she had the support of her family, it took Debra's forceful personality to get through those first years. There were city and

CAREER CHECKLIST ✔

You'll like this job if you ...

- Are interested in eating well and staying fit, so you'll have the stamina to do the hard work needed

- Can follow projects through to the end

- Like things very clean

- Have an eye for detail

- Are willing to listen to people to see what they want and need

- Love food

- Will learn how to sell and market your products

GROUNDBREAKERS

Retail Clerks' Union
Vice President

Mary Burke was elected vice president of the retail clerks union in 1888. United Food and Commercial Waiters International Union was created in 1979 when two unions merged—Retail Clerks and Amalgamated Meat Cutters. Today the UFCWI has 600 local unions and encourages women to take leadership roles. The UFCWI union has 1.4 million members in the United States and Canada. Some 50 percent are women working in grocery stores, meat and food processing plants, department stores, and hospitals.

Source: *The Reader's Companion to Women's History*. (1998). NY: Houghton Mifflin

county regulations to be contended with, long hours to be worked, and few customers. Because there was a kitchen on premises, many of the regulations for restaurants had to be followed, and some of them were not good for a natural foods store. For example, the Board of Health wanted Debra to spray for bugs in the kitchen once a month. Finally, she convinced them that natural traps would be as effective and followed her philosophy of natural foods.

Her Business Expands

Gradually, people in the area began to realize what a great store Debra was running. They began asking for advice about how to eat well to prevent health problems. As sales increased and her store expanded, Debra needed people to help her with the day-to-day business. Usually she didn't find them; they found her through their interest in natural foods. Today, Debra has people to help stock the store, to wait on customers, and to run the cash registers. One of her employees is a nurse. Another owned a health food store in Seattle. Once the people started helping, Debra could spend more time on food products and was able to create and perfect the granola.

Today Debra has more time to spend marketing her store's products and marketing and selling her granola, which has now been placed with two major West Coast distributors. Debra is also the author of two cookbooks, which she originally self-published, but now publishes through a publishing company. She also writes an advice newsletter and calendar for her customers, telling them when free talks will be held at the store (some evenings and Saturdays).

Debra is preparing for a cooking show on public television. Just as with everything else in her food career, the cooking show will be an uphill battle. She will have to find the sponsors and help promote the show to an audience. She'll have help from her brother, a television producer.

Debra believes in sharing as much information as possible with the people who work with her, so that they can see how to do things better. She tries to share as much as she can about what she's learned—about food and nutrition, about business, and about teaching people to eat right—with her employees, who are also her friends. She also shares the profits with the rest of the workers in the store.

(in disguise)

Phyllis Richman

Phyllis Richman

Special Columnist, *The Washington Post*, The
Washington Post Company, Washington, DC

Major in American Studies

Restaurant Critic

Dining Advice from a Gourmet

Phyllis Richman created a career out of two of her favorite activities: writing and eating. Phyllis is the restaurant critic for *The Washington Post*. People read her restaurant reviews to find out where to go for dinner, to get ideas for new ways to prepare food, and to be entertained. Phyllis also writes a dining guide, teaches food writing, and is a mystery novelist. In her first mystery, *The Butter Did It*, a restaurant critic discovers who killed her good friend, a great chef. Her second mystery, *Murder on the Gravy Train*, continues the detective career of her restaurant critic heroine.

Writing about a restaurant can be the most fun or the dreariest part of a restaurant critic's job, Phyllis says. But going to a new restaurant is

FOOD WRITER

Salaries for food writers are related to the size of the publication, geographic area, and whether the writer is covered by a union contract. Writers whose work is syndicated earn extra money because their work appears in many publications.

- Entry level average $300 week
- Experienced $1,000 a week and up

Source: Encyclopedia of Careers and Vocational Guidance

PHYLLIS' CAREER PATH

Writes for essay contests and local newspapers

Cooks interesting food at home

Graduates college

always exciting. Before writing a restaurant review, Phyllis visits a restaurant anonymously two or three times and observes and analyzes the service, the atmosphere, and of course, the food. She usually invites others to join her for lunch or dinner. In that way she can taste a number of different dishes—her friends' and her own selections. When she is sure that she has enough information to write a

from 3 hours to 3 days to write, depending on how clear I am about what I think, whether there is an obvious story to tell, and what differentiates the restaurant from others," she says. Her reviews are published once a week in *The Washington Post* newspaper's Sunday magazine.

Sometimes she writes pieces for other sections of the newspaper, usually about food. Occasionally, she will

> # The important thing is perseverance. If I saw a job I wanted I just kept at it and kept at it until I got it.

fair critique, she sits down at her computer and tells the world what she thinks about the restaurant.

"My reviews will take anywhere

travel to other parts of the country to do food stories, and once in a while she travels to Europe.

Every Fall she teaches a course on

Works as city
▼ planner

Freelances, writing
▼ about food

Joins Post as
▼ restaurant critic

newspaper and magazine food writing at the Culinary Institute of America in California. She plans to write a mystery book each year now, writing at home, rather than the office, where most of her writing is done. She is lucky enough to have her own office at the *Post*. Most of the writers at the *Post* are in a room with many other writers. But because she a columnist and does not "belong" to any section of the paper, she has a separate office.

Phyllis enjoys and appreciates restaurants. She loves to eat, and she appreciates food as an art. She also loves the business and society of restaurants, restaurants as a cultural force, and restaurants as a social form. But, she says, the challenges are writing on demand, writing the same kinds of things, and finding new ways of saying the same or similar things. "You can't write for a million people," she says, "so you have to write for yourself, with some awareness of which restaurants would appeal to which types of people."

Loves to Read

From a very young age, this restaurant critic loved to read. She would enter essay contests as a teenager. She also worked for neighborhood newspapers. Her favorite subjects in school were English and math, and she didn't like home economics. "It was stifling," she says.

Phyllis began her writing career as a freelance writer. While she loved to write as a child and in college, she did not do much writing during the first 10 years after she graduated from college. She got her degree in American Studies from Brandeis University in Boston and then got a job as a city planner. She married young, and had three children right away. In her early 30s, she was raising kids and going to graduate school, studying sociology. But she began doing freelance writing, and found that more interesting and financially rewarding than her school work. She decided to leave school and concentrate on writing for a living.

"The first thing I did was to find a weekly newspaper that was looking for a restaurant critic, and I tried out for that job. Once I found that I could do that, I sent things to local publications and then moved up to national magazines and got my feet wet there. It was very useful to have local outlets, so that when an editor needed something he might think of me. I developed a reputation for being reliable, on time, and a good writer, just kind of building the editor's confidence in me."

A Washington, DC native, Phyllis first wrote for local Washington newspapers and magazines. During her freelance career, she had the discipline and tenacity to keep sending out her work, even when she was rejected. After 4 years she was making an excellent living doing food writing—

producing more than 200 pieces a year. When the *Post* offered her a job as food critic on staff, she had to take a cut in pay but decided it was a good career move. She has worked at the *Post* for 22 years.

"It's very nice to be working for a big company that has the resources that allow you to best do your job by visiting a restaurant several times to effectively critique it. At a small paper where funds are limited and they can't afford to spend very much, it makes it harder to do a good job. But if you want to be a food critic today, that's probably where you will have to start."

CAREER CHECKLIST ✔

You'll like this job if you ...

- Love to read and to write

- Will learn about different types of food

- Are interested in describing food

- Can go the extra mile to check all your facts

- Like to eat

- Have the patience and discipline to keep trying even if people reject your work

Stardust Restaurant, Alexandria, VA

GROUNDBREAKERS

African American Catering Pioneers

The catering business was historically the most successful early business venture for African Americans and the credit belongs to women, who were the first to enter the business. Among the most notable was Cornelia Gomez, who did catering in New York somewhere between 1780 and 1820. Her successor was Katie Ferguson, who kept the business until about 1820.

Others identified are Mrs. Henry F. Jones of Philadelphia and Julia Wyche Boggs, originally from Henderson, North Carolina, who became a successful caterer in Washington, DC, after working in private homes for a number of years.

In Omaha, Nebraska, Helen Mahamitt and her husband founded a catering business in 1905. She studied at (Fannie) Farmer's School in Boston and at one of the finest school in Paris, France, in 1927. She taught advanced cooking and catering in a private school which she organized—the only school of its kind west of Chicago.

Source: *Contributions of Black Women to America* (Vol. 1). (1982). Columbia, SC: Kenday Press.

In her first years at the *Post*, Phyllis wrote restaurant reviews and articles exclusively about food. Then she was "promoted" and she also acted as the editor of the paper's food section. But she didn't enjoy managing as much as writing, so she negotiated a new job so that she could leave the editing and managing job and spend more time writing, She developed a syndicated newspaper column, which she wrote for many years, and placed articles in other national publications. She invented a guide that she calls her *50 Favorite Restaurants*, which takes her about 9 months to complete. "I don't try to cover all the restaurants in Washington, DC," she says. "That would be too hard. So I call it my 50 favorite, rather than the 50 best." Phyllis starts with about 100 restaurants that she likes, and visits them to narrow her choices down to the 50 she thinks are most deserving.

A new responsibility has been added to her job this year—a "chat group" where readers can ask questions through the *Post*'s Web site. "We're trying that for a year and it's fun. Some of the questions I get from readers are interesting. I choose the ones I want to answer. I don't want to answer questions about where to go to dinner Saturday night. I look for ones that will encourage conversation with allow me enough time to do some of the things I love, such as going to the theater or musical concerts." On vacations, she enjoys cooking or going to restaurants that aren't very fancy, reading and watching movies.

No matter what kind of writer you are, you have to be accurate, be willing to go through the trouble to find out that every detail is right. Check every detail to make sure you find out as whole a truth as you can.

my readers, things like what is happening with local restaurants, procedures for tipping, and questions about reviewing restaurants—questions that are more conversational than specific. Then I encourage others to post their opinions."

Most of Phyllis' life is taken up with writing. "This job doesn't really

Stardust Restaurant, Alexandria, VA

Getting Started On Your

Own Career Path

Getting Started On Your Own Career Path

WHAT TO DO NOW

To help you prepare for a career in food, the women interviewed for this book recommend things you can do now, while still in school.

Susan Spicer, Chef, Restaurant and Cooking School Owner

Be willing to taste lots of things. Try things out in your kitchen. If someone in the family likes to cook, ask to help them.

In school, pay attention to math—you'll need it in proportioning, portion control, and figuring out how to multiply recipes—and English—you'll need to know how to compose a menu, how to spell and write descriptions that flow nicely.

Study another language so that you can work in another country. I would not have gotten half my experience in France had I not spoken decent French.

Get experience first before you commit to a culinary school, so you'll know if this work is something you'll like. All cooking jobs aren't in restaurants—there are cruise ships, institutional kitchens, food styling, food journalism, and being a personal chef.

Ann Cashion, Chef, Restaurant Owner

The most important part of becoming a great chef is something nobody can teach you. It's learning to discriminate while eating, paying attention to what you eat, trying to have as many experiences with food as you can. Some people who want to cook want to learn a lot, but there is a big gap in their eating background. You can teach someone the skills of cooking, what ingredients to put in, but in order to teach them how to season for taste, they have to have an educated palate.

Julie Simonson, Food Scientist

Experiment at home. Play around in the kitchen. I did a lot of cooking at home and just learned what works and what doesn't. I am very comfortable at cooking.

I highly encourage you to get involved in organizations and take a leadership role. I was in 4-H. I started out as historian and then moved up the ladder to secretary, and finally to president of the local club. Then I went on to the county 4-H council.

Be involved in math and science classes. They are the foundation for this type of work. Take microbiology as soon as you can.

Mary Maczko, Military Food Service

You have to really want to be a cook to do this. It's not an easy job. You have to just follow your vision and stick with it.

Bonnie Johnson Alton, Bread Store Owner

Spend time in your kitchen. Try making four small pieces instead of one large one loaf. Do different things to each piece—under knead, over knead, add flavor—then bake it and see what the consequences are.

Eat discriminately and develop your taste. You will soon understand what flavors go well together, like the difference between basil and thyme and basil and oregano.

Julia Iantosca, Winemaker

Pursue math and science courses in junior high and high school. That is the core education you will need. In college I had math all the way through calculus, also physics, chemistry courses through biochemistry, and my microbiology courses, similar to a pre-med or a biology major.

Paula Lambert, Cheesemaker Entrepreneur

Try to get a volunteer job or offer to help someone doing something that interests you. Try it out to see if you really like it.

Studying a foreign language is a good idea. It will always help you later on. In my case, I needed those foreign languages to learn cheesemaking from the best.

RECOMMENDED READING

Cookbooks

As any visit to a book store or the library will show you, there are far too many cookbooks for us to list them. But we've mentioned a few you might find interesting, and the most popular as mentioned by experts in the field.

The All-Purpose Cookbook *Joy of Cooking* by Irma von Starkloff Rombauer and Marion Rombauer Becker. (1975) NY: Bobbs-Merrill; reprinted 1997 by Plume.

The All New All Purpose *Joy of Cooking* by Irma von Starkloff Rombauer, Marion Rombauer Becker, and Ethan Becker. (1997). NY: Scribner.

Mastering the Art of French Cooking by Julia Child

The Little House Cooking Book: Frontier Foods from Laura Ingalls Wilder's Classic Stories by Barbara Walker. (1979). NY: Harper & Row.

Other cookbooks with familiar characters: Winnie the Pooh, Paddington, Anne of Green Gables, Mary Poppins, American Girl characters.

Biography:

Appetite for Life, Biography of Julia Child by Noel Riley Fitch. (1997). NY: Doubleday.

Stand Facing the Stove: The Story of the Women Who Gave America the Joy of Cooking, by Anne Mendelson. (1996). NY H. Hold.

Epicurean Delight: The Life and Times of James Beard by Evan Jones. (1990). NY: Knopf.

Murder Mysteries

The much-loved chef turned detective Eugenia Potter in *Cooking School Murders*, *Baked Bean Supper Murders*, *Nantucket Diet Murders* by Virginia Rich.

Caterer Goldie Bear solves mysteries in *Dying for Chocolate*, *Killer Pancakes*, *Cereal Murders*, and others by Diane Mott Davidson.

Kate Cavenaugh, caters parties, travels, and solves murders in *Beat a Rotten Egg* by Cathie John, Cathie Celestri, John Celestri.

Restaurant critic turns detective in *The Butter Did It* by Phyllis Richman.

Other Selections

Recipes and profiles of famous women chefs. *Women of Taste* by Beverly Russell (Editor). (1997). NY: John Wiley & Sons.

How the best in the business got where they are today, plus recipes. *On Becoming a Chef* by Andrew Dornenburg, Karen Page. (1995). John Wiley & Sons.

A Woman's Place Is in the Kitchen: The Evolution of Women Chefs by Ann Cooper. (1997). John Wiley & Sons.

Through the Kitchen Window: Women Writers Celebrate Food and Cooking by Arlene Voski Avakian (Editor). (1997). Beacon Press.

General References

Encyclopedia of Career and Vocational Guidance. (1997). Chicago: J. G. Ferguson

Peterson's Scholarships, Grants, and Prizes. (1997). Princeton, NJ: Peterson's.

web site: www.petersons.com

The Girls' Guide to Life How to Take Charge of the Issues that Affect You by Catherine Dee. (1997). Boston: Little, Brown & Co.

Celebrates achievements of girls and women, extensive resources

PROFESSIONAL GROUPS

Many food groups have their own organization and website. Check these groups and others for career exploration information, local student chapters, scholarships, and study guidelines. For additional organizations, check your library for the *Encyclopedia of Associations*, published by Gale Research.

American Cheese Society

Promotes all kinds of cheese, holds conferences and competitions.

    P. O. Box 303, Delavan, WI 53115-0303

    (414) 728-4458

American Institute of Baking

    1213 Bakers Way, Manhattan, KS 66502

    (785) 537-4750

American Wine Society

Founded 1967, this group promotes the appreciate of wine through education. It has many local chapter groups.

    3006 Latta Rd., Rochester, NY 14612-3298

Culinary Institute of America

Oldest culinary college in the United States. Provides continuing and advanced professional educational training in the food, wine, and hospitality fields at its two campuses.

    Route 9, Hyde Park, NY

    (800) 285-4627; (914) 471-6608

    website: www.ciachef.edu

2555 Main St. (at Greystone), St. Helena, CA 94574

(707) 967-0600

International Association of Culinary Professionals

This educational-type group gives the Julia Child Cookbook Awards and awards scholarships and research grants through its Foundation.

304 West Liberty St., Ste. 201, Louisville, KY 40202

(502) 581-9786

1-800-928-4227

website: www.iacp-online.org

International Association of Women Chefs and Restauranteurs

This group promotes education and advancement for women and its members compete for scholarships.

304 West Liberty St., Ste. 201, Louisville, KY 40202

(502) 581-0300

website: www.chefnet.com/wci

James Beard Foundation

American's only historical culinary center, this organization is headquartered in Beard's restored brownstone home in Greenwich Village, New York. Meals are prepared there, and the organization offers scholarships and publications.

167 W. 12th St., New York, NY 10011

(212) 675-4984

website: www.jamesbeard.org

Les Dames d'Escoffier International

Founded in 1976 and named for the famous French chef Auguste Escoffier, LDEI has 19 chapters in the United States, Canada and Australia. Members are professional women in fields of food, wine, hospitality, and the arts of the table. Has scholarship and grant programs.

P. O. Box 2103, Reston, VA 20195-0103

(703) 716-5913

How COOL Are You?!

Cool girls like to DO things, not just sit around like couch potatoes. There are many things you can get involved in now to benefit your future. Some cool girls even know what careers they want (or think they want).

Not sure what you want to do? That's fine, too... the Cool Careers series for Girls can help you explore lots of careers with a number of great, easy to use tools! Learn where to go and to whom you should talk about different careers, as well as books to read and videos to see. Then, you're on the road to cool girl success!

Written especially for girls, this new series tells what it's like today for women in all types of jobs with special emphasis on nontraditional careers for women. The upbeat and informative pages provide answers to questions you want answered, such as:

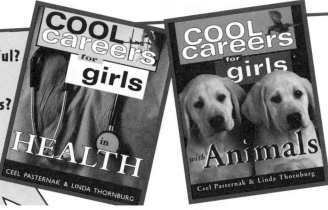

- ✔ **What jobs do women find meaningful?**
- ✔ **What do women succeed at today?**
- ✔ **How did they prepare for these jobs?**
- ✔ **How did they find their job?**
- ✔ **What are their lives like?**
- ✔ **How do I find out more about this type of work?**

Each book profiles ten women who love their work. These women had dreams, but didn't always know what they wanted to be when they grew up. Zoologist Claudia Luke knew she wanted to work outdoors and that she was interested in animals, but she didn't even know what a zoologist was, much less what they did and how you got to be one. Elizabeth Gruben was going to be a lawyer until she discovered the world of Silicon Valley computers and started her own multimedia company. Mary Beth Quinn grew up in Stowe, Vermont, where she skied competitively and taught skiing. Now she runs a ski school at a Virginia ski resort. These three women's stories appear with others in a new series of career books for young readers.

The Cool Careers for Girls series encourages career exploration and broadens girls' career horizons. It shows girls what it takes to succeed, by providing easy-to-read information about careers that young girls may not have considered because they didn't know about them. They learn from women who are in today's workplace—women who know what it takes today to get the job.

ORDER FORM

Title	Paper	Cloth	Quantity
Cool Careers for Girls in Computers	$12.95	$19.95	_____
Cool Careers for Girls in Sports	$12.95	$19.95	_____
Cool Careers for Girls with Animals	$12.95	$19.95	_____
Cool Careers for Girls in Health	$12.95	$19.95	_____
Cool Careers for Girls in Engineering	$12.95	$19.95	_____
Cool Careers for Girls with Food	$12.95	$19.95	_____
	SUBTOTAL		_____

VA Residents add 4½ % sales tax
Shipping/handling $5.00+ $5.00
$1.50 for each additional book order (__ x $1.50)

TOTAL ENCLOSED   _____

SHIP TO: (street address only for UPS or RPS delivery)
Name: _____
Address: _____

☐ I enclose check/money order for $ ____ made payable to Impact Publications
☐ Charge $ ____ to: ☐ Visa ☐ MasterCard ☐ AmEx ☐ Discover

Card #: _____ Expiration: _____
Signature: _____ Phone number: _____

Phone toll-free at 1-800/361-1055, or fax/mail/email your order to:
Impact Publications
9104-N Manassas Drive, Manassas Park, VA 20111-5211
Fax: 703/335-9486; email: orders@impactpublications.com